Our Common Land

OUR COMMON LAND

(AND OTHER SHORT ESSAYS).

BY

OCTAVIA HILL.

London:

MACMILLAN AND CO.

1877.

CHARLES DICKENS AND EVANS,
CRYSTAL PALACE PRESS.

CONTENTS.

OUR COMMON LAND.

PROBABLY few persons who have a choice of holidays select a Bank holiday, which falls in the spring or summer, as one on which they will travel, or stroll in the country, unless, indeed, they live in neighbourhoods very far removed from large towns. Every railway station is crowded; every booking-office thronged; every seat—nay, all standing room—is occupied in every kind of public conveyance; the roads leading out of London for miles are crowded with every description of vehicle—van, cart, chaise, gig—drawn by every size and sort of donkey, pony, or horse; if it be a dusty day, a great dull unbroken choking cloud of dust hangs over every line of road.

B

Yet in spite of all this, and in spite of the
really bad sights to be seen at every public-
house on the road, in spite of the wild songs
and boisterous behaviour, and reckless driving
home at night, which show how sadly intoxi-
cation is still bound up with the idea and
practical use of a holiday to hundreds of our
people, how much intense enjoyment the day
gives! how large a part of this enjoyment is
unmixed good! And the evil is kept in check
very much. We may see the quiet figure of
the mounted policeman as we drive home,
dark in the twilight, dark amidst the dust,
keeping order among the vehicles, making
the drunken drivers mind what they are doing.
He keeps very tolerable order. And then
these days in the country ought to lessen the
number of drunkards every year; and more
and more we shall be able to trust to the
public opinion of the quiet many to preserve
order.

And watch, when at last the open spaces

are reached towards which all these lines of
vehicles are tending—be it Epping, or Richmond, or Greenwich, or Hampstead—every
place seems swarming with an undisciplined,
but heartily happy, crowd. The swings, the
roundabouts, the donkeys, the stalls, are beset
by dozens or even hundreds of pleasure-seekers,
gay and happy, though they are not always
the gentlest or most refined. Look at the
happy family groups—father, and mother, and
children, with their picnic dinners neatly tied
up in handkerchiefs; watch the joy of eager
children leaning out of vans to purchase for
a halfpenny the wonderful pink paper streamers
which they will stick proudly in their caps;
see the merry little things running untiringly
up and down the bank of sand or grass;
notice the affectionate father bringing out the
pot of ale to the wife as she sits comfortably
tucked up in shawls in the little cart, or
treating the children to sweetmeats; sym-
pathise in the hearty energy of the great

rough lads who have walked miles, as their
dusty boots well show; their round, honest
faces have beamed with rough mirth at every
joke that has come in their way all day;
they have rejoiced more in the clamber to
obtain the great branches of may than even
in the proud possession of them, though they
are carrying them home in triumph. To all
these the day brings unmixed good.

Now, have you ever paused to think what
Londoners would do without this holiday, or
what it would be without these open spaces?
Cooped up for many weeks in close rooms, in
narrow streets, compelled on their holiday to
travel for miles in a crowded stream, first between houses, and then between dusty high
hedges, suddenly they expand into free un-
crowded space under spreading trees, or on
to the wide Common from which blue distance
is visible; the eye, long unrefreshed with sight
of growing grass, or star-like flowers, is rejoiced by them again. To us the Common

or forest looks indeed crowded with people, but
to them the feeling is one of sufficient space,
free air, green grass, and colour, with a life
without which they might think the place
dull. Every atom of open space you have
left to these people is needed; take care you
lose none of it; it is becoming yearly of more
vital importance to save or increase it.

There is now a Bill for regulating inclosure
before the House of Commons. Mr. Cross
has said what he trusts will be its effect if it
becomes law; but those who have been watching the history of various inclosures, and the
trials respecting special Commons, are not so
hopeful as Mr. Cross is as to the effect this
Bill would have. It makes indeed good provisions for regulating Commons to be kept
open for the public when a scheme for regulation is applied for. But the adoption of
such a scheme depends in large part on the
lord of the manor. Will he in nine cases out
of ten ever even apply for a scheme for regu-

lating a Common, when he knows that by
doing so he shuts out from himself and his
successors for ever the possibility of inclosing
it, and appropriating some part of it? Do any
provisions for regulating, however excellent,
avail anything when no motive exists which
should prompt the lord of the manor to bring
the Common under them? and, as the Bill
stands, it cannot be so brought without his
consent.

Secondly, the Bill provides that urban sanitary authorities can purchase rights which
will enable them to keep open any suburban
Common, or may accept a gift of the same.
But then a suburban Common is defined as
one situated within six miles of the outside
of a town of 5,000 inhabitants. Now, I hardly
know how far out of a large town Bank-
holiday excursionists go, but I know they go
every year farther and farther. I am sure
that a Common twelve, nay, twenty, miles off
from a large town is accessible by cheap trains

to hundreds of excursionists all the summer, to whom it is an inestimable boon. Again, is the privilege of space, and light, and air, and beauty not to be considered for the small shop-keeper, for the hard-working clerk, who will probably never own a square yard of English land, but who cares to take his wife and children into the country for a fortnight in the summer? Do you not know numbers of neigh-bourhoods where woods, and Commons, and fields used to be open to pedestrians, and now they must walk, even in the country, on straight roads between hedges? The more that fields and woods are closed, the more does every atom of Common land, everywhere, all over England, become of importance to the people of every class, except that which owns its own parks and woods. "On the lowest computation," says the Report of the Com-mons Preservation Society, "5,000,000 acres of Common land have been inclosed since Queen Anne's reign; now there are but

1,000,000 acres left.* The right of roving over
these lands has been an immense boon to our
people ; it becomes at once more valued and
rarer year by year. Is it impossible, I would
ask lawyers and statesmen, to recognise this
right as a legal one acquired by custom, and
not to be taken away ? Mr. Lefevre suggested
this in a letter to *The Times.* He says:

"The right of the public to use and enjoy
Commons (which they have for centuries exer-
cised), it must be admitted, is not distinctly
recognised by law, though there is a remarkable absence of adverse testimony on the subject. The law, however, most fully recognises
the right of the village to its green, and allows
the establishment of such right by evidence
as to playing games, &c., but it has failed as

* The amount remaining uninclosed and subject to Common-
rights is variously estimated ; a report of the Inclosure Commissioners in 1874 putting it at about 2,600,000 for England and
Wales, while the recent return of landowners, prepared by the
Local Government Board, makes the uninclosed area little
more than 1,500,000 acres.

yet to recognise the analogy between the great
town and its Common, and the village and
its green, however complete in fact that
analogy may be. But some of these rights of
Common, which are now so prized as a means
of keeping Commons open, had, if legal theory
is correct, their origin centuries ago in custom.
For long they had no legal existence, but the
courts of law at last learned to recognise custom as conferring rights. The custom has
altered in kind; in lieu of cattle, sheep, and
pigs turned out to pasture on the Commons,
human beings have taken their place, and
wear down the turf instead of eating it. I
can see no reason why the law, or, if the
courts are too slow to move, the Legislature,
should not recognise this transfer and legalise
this custom. Again, it is probable that Commons belonged originally much more to the inhabitants of a district than to the lord. Feudal
theory and its subsequent development—English Real Property Law—have ridden rather

roughly over the facts and the rights of the
case. The first placed the lord of the manor
in his position as lord, giving him certain
privileges, and coupling with them many responsibilities. The second gradually removed
these responsibilities, and converted into a
property what was at first little more than an
official trust. If these considerations are beyond the scope of the law courts, they are
proper for Parliament. One step has been
made. It has been proved that it is not
necessary to purchase Commons for the public,
but that ample means of protecting them from
inclosure exist. It is also obvious that the
rights which constitute these means are now
in practice represented by a public user of
Commons for recreation. The Legislature
should, I venture to think, recognise this user
as a legal right."

If the Legislature would do this, Commons
all over England might be kept open, which,
I venture to think, would be a great gain.

Hitherto the right to keep Commons open has been maintained, even in the neighbourhood of towns, by legal questions affecting rights of pasturage, of cutting turf, or carting gravel. This is all very well if it secures the object, but it is on the large ground of public policy, for the sake of the health and enjoyment of the people, that the conscience of the nation supports the attempt to keep them open ; it cares little for the defence of obsolete and often nearly valueless customs, and it would be very well if the right acquired by use could be recognised by law, and the defence put at once on its real grounds.

I have referred to the opinion expressed by lawyers and members of Parliament that the opportunity of applying for schemes for regulation provided by the Bill now before the House will not be used at all largely, owing to the necessity of the consent of those owning two-thirds value of the Common, and of the veto possessed by the lord of the manor.

They tell me also (and it certainly appears to
me that both statements are evident on reading
the Bill) that *unless Mr. Cross consents to
insert a clause forbidding all inclosures except
under this Act*, the passing of it will be fol-
lowed by a large number of high-handed
inclosures under old Acts, or without legal
right. For unless the right of some independent body like the public who use the
space can be recognised as having a voice
in opposing illegal inclosures, what chance
have the rural Commons? The agricultural
labourers, often tenants-at-will of a powerful
landlord, can be ejected and their rights immediately cancelled ; moreover, they do not
know the law, they have few to advise them,
to plead their cause, or to spend money on
expensive lawsuits. Mr. Lefevre says in the
same letter quoted above, "I would at least
ask them to declare all inclosures not authorised by Parliament to be *primâ facie* illegal
and to remove the necessity of litigation by

persons actually themselves commoners, by
authorising any public body, or public-spirited
individual, to interfere in the case of any such
inclosures, and put the lord to strict proof of
his right."

And do not let us be too ready to see the
question dealt with as a matter of mere money
compensation. It is much to be feared lest
the short-sighted cupidity of one generation
of rural commoners may lose a great possession for future times. This danger is im-
minent because we are all so accustomed to
treat money value as if it were the only real
value! Can we wonder if the eyes of poor
men are often fixed rather on the immediate
money value to themselves than on the effect
of changes for their descendants? Should we
stand by, we who ought to see farther, and
let them part with what ought to be a possession to the many in the future? A few
coals at Christmas, which rapidly come to be
looked upon as a charity graciously accorded

by the rich, or the recipients of which are
arbitrarily selected by them, may in many
cases be blindly accepted by cottagers in lieu
of Common rights. Is the influence of such
doles so healthy that we should wish to see
them taking the place of a Common right
over a little bit of English soil? The issue
at a nominal charge of orders to cut turf or
furze by a lord of the manor has been known
gradually to extinguish the right to do so
without his leave. Is the influence of the
rich and powerful so slight that we should
let it be thus silently strengthened? Is the
knowledge just brought so prominently before
us that one quarter of the land in England
is owned by only seven hundred and ten
persons so satisfactory that we will stand by
and see quietly absorbed those few spots which
are our common birthright in the soil? It
is not likely that farms or estates will diminish
in size; and the yeoman class is, I suppose,
passing away rapidly. With the small hold-

ings, is there to pass away from our people
the sense that they have any share in the
soil of their native England? I think the
sense of owning some spaces of it in common may be healthier for them than even the
possession of small bits by individuals, and
certainly it now seems more feasible. Lowell
tells us that what is free to all is the best
of all possessions :

> 'Tis heaven alone that is given away,
> 'Tis only God may be had for the asking ;
> There is no price set on the lavish summer,
> And June may be had by the poorest comer.

Hugh Miller, too, points out how intimately
the right to roam over the land is connected
with the love of it, and hence with patriotism.
He says, speaking of his first visit to Edin-
burgh : "I threw myself, as usual, for com-
pensatory pleasures, on my evening walks,
but found the inclosed state of the district,
and the fence of a rigorously-administered
trespass-law, serious drawbacks; and ceased to

wonder that a thoroughly cultivated country is, in most instances, so much less beloved by its people than a wild and open one. Rights of proprietorship may exist equally in both; but there is an important sense in which the open country belongs to the proprietors and to the people too. All that the heart and intellect can derive from it may be alike free to peasant and aristocrat; whereas the cultivated and strictly fenced country belongs usually, in every sense, to only the proprietor; and as it is a much simpler and more obvious matter to love one's country as a scene of hills, and streams, and green fields, amid which nature has often been enjoyed, than as a definite locality, in which certain laws and constitutional privileges exist, it is rather to be regretted than wondered at that there should be often less true patriotism in a country of just institutions and equal laws, whose soil has been so exclusively appropriated as to leave only the dusty high-roads to its people, than in wild open countries, in which the popular mind and affections are left free to embrace the soil, but whose institutions are partial and defective." So writes at least one man of the people; and whether we estimate the relative value of just laws or familiar and beloved scenes quite as he does, or not, I think we must all feel there is deep truth in what he says.

Let us then press Government, while there is still time, that no bit of the small portion of uninclosed ground, which is the common inheritance of us all as English men and women, shall be henceforth inclosed, except under this Bill; which simply means that each scheme shall be submitted to a Committee of the House, and considered on its merits.

Surely this is a very reasonable request. Do not let us be satisfied with less. Do not let us deceive ourselves as to the result of this Bill if it pass unamended.

c

II.

DISTRICT VISITING.*

I HAVE assumed throughout this paper that most district visitors feel a certain dissatisfaction both with district visiting and with systems of relief as they exist, even where such systems are best organised. Some may think that there is too much relief given, some that there is too little, others that what is given is of the wrong kind. I believe, also, some visitors feel that their spiritual influence is interfered with in different ways by the unsatisfactory character of the temporal relief. To some of them it

---

* Read on the 4th of May, 1876, to a meeting of district visitors and clergy at the Bishop of Gloucester and Bristol's house in London.

seems incongruous to carry tracts in one hand and coal-tickets in another ; to others, that carrying either, still more carrying both, as a matter of course, shuts them off from true intercourse with the best kind of working men and women ; others, again, feel that carrying tracts without coal-tickets when the grate is empty seems a little like want of sympathy ; and others that carrying coal-tickets without tracts is treating the poor as if they were only concerned with the outside things of life.

However earnestly our clergy have desired to solve this problem of how to deal wisely with the temporal condition of their flocks, it remains a problem still. However tenderly our visitors have mourned over it, as it affects hundreds of individuals, it remains mournful still. What prospect is there of its being vigorously studied with a view to solution, or even to radical improvement, by those who have power to effect improvement ? Busy, overworked clergymen, with services and sermons, and churches

and schools, and thousands of souls to see to,
have inherited systems of relief in their parishes
which they hardly have time to reform, and
the gigantic pressure of daily duty perpetuates
many unwise plans, though many, I am well
aware, are being abolished.   How far the best
still falls below what they would like to see
let the clergy themselves say.   I believe most
of them, if asked, would reply : " I have tried
honestly to make my system of relief as satisfactory as I could, but it is far from my ideal."
And this is so from another cause.   You can
never make a *system* of relief good without
perfect administration, far-sighted watchfulness
in each individual case ; and this is specially
true in an age in which bad systems of relief
have trained the people to improvidence.   Given
your entirely enlightened clergyman, he cannot
in a large London parish do much more than
see to his people when the crisis of distress has
come.   He cannot watch over them before it
comes, yet it is then that distress is preventable.

On whom does the continuous watchfulness devolve at best? Visitors, young, inexperienced, untaught, undertake districts ; they find themselves part of a system, and follow in its lines ; they meet individual cases of want, improvidence, disease, and though they know little themselves how to deal with such, they hesitate to make calls upon the time of a too busy clergyman, kind as he is in helping, gladly as he would reply to a practical question about the individual ; they cannot talk out with him radical means of dealing with the roots of such evils. What can they do ? They give or withhold the soup-ticket or the shilling. Has the clergyman usually time, has the visitor often knowledge to do much more than deal with the individual question of relief or no relief at the moment in the special case ?

And yet the problem has become appalling, gigantic : viewed in its entirety, it might make us almost tremble ?

Statesmen, philanthropists, political econo-

mists, try their hands at it, or rather their
heads. Do they succeed better than the clergy
and the visitors? Do they not often succeed
worse? For the clergy and the visitors at
least bear witness to the poor of sympathy
with them, and deal with the wants round
them practically; while the theorists, let their
theories be ever so excellent, somehow stand
so far off that they bring little practically into
operation. Who does not know of good laws
passed which are nearly inoperative because
not enforced by brave persons face to face with
the evils which should be removed by them?
Who does not know of sound principles of
political economy clearly enunciated to those
unconcerned by them, which never reach the
ears of those whose lives they deeply affect,
still less are brought before them by those
whom they would trust?

Now these two classes, the studious, more
leisurely, generalising thinkers, and the loving,
individualising doers, need to be brought into

communication ; and that is what in this paper
I wish most emphatically to enforce. Each
has knowledge the other requires ; separated,
they are powerless ; combined, they may do
much. For I have drawn miserable pictures
of the weakness of both, but see on the other
hand what each has of strength. The clergy
have all that is pitiful, all that is generous in
the hearts of their richer parishioners on their
side—the power of calling out workers from
among them, the power of directing a large
part of their alms, the distribution of money,
the leadership of the men. Besides these they
have the enormous accumulated knowledge of
the poor, gathered in long years of intimate
observation of them in their homes—a mass
of information over which they may not have
much time to brood, and from which they may
not be in the habit of generalising, yet what
might not the theorists learn from it?

And the visitors. I have called them inexperienced, and I might have added that their

work is less valuable in many ways, because it is intermittent; but pause to think what these visitors are and might be. Hundreds, perhaps thousands, of gentle, earnest, duty-doing souls, well born, well nurtured, well provided for, possibly well educated, turning aside out of the bright paths which they could pursue continuously, to bring a little joy, a little help, to those who are out of the way. A voluntary gift this, if a very solemn duty. I have heard persons who give their whole time to the poor speak a little disparagingly of these fleeting visits, and young girls themselves, fevered with desire to do more, talk rather enviously of those who can give their time wholly to such work; but have they ever thought how much is lost by such entire dedication?—or, rather, how much is gained by her who is not only a visitor of the poor, but a member of a family with other duties? It is the families, the homes of the poor, that need to be influenced. Is not she most sympathetic, most powerful, who nursed her own mother through her long illness, and knew how to go quietly about the darkened room; who entered so heartily into the sister's love and marriage; who obeyed so perfectly the father's command when it was hardest? Better still if she be wife and mother herself, and can enter into the responsibilities of a head of a household, understands her joys and cares, knows what heroic patience it needs to keep gentle when the nerves are unhinged and the children noisy. Depend upon it, if we thought of the poor primarily as husbands, wives, sons, and daughters, members of households, as we are ourselves, instead of contemplating them as a different class, we should recognise better how the house training and high ideal of home duty was our best preparation for work among them. Nay, to come down to much smaller matters than these family duties, to the gladness of party, ball, and flower-show, I believe these, too, in innocent and happy amount, when they brighten

the eyes and bring the ready smile to the face,
and make the step free and joyous, prepare us
to bring a gleam of sunlight into many a
monotonous life among the poor. What, in
comparison with these gains, is the regularity
of work of the weary worker, whose life tends
to make her deal with people *en masse*, who
gains little fresh spring from other thoughts
and scenes ? For what is it that we look
forward to as our people gradually improve ?
Not surely to dealing with them as a class at
all, any more than we should tell ourselves
off to labour for the middle class, or aristo-
cratic class, or shop-keeping class. Our ideal
must be to promote the happy natural intercourse of neighbours — mutual knowledge,
mutual help, of a kind, certainly, but not this
professed devotion of a life ; and it will be
better from the beginning to mould our system
so that it shall bear witness of what it ought
to become. If we establish a system of professed workers, amateur or paid, we shall

quickly begin to hug our system, and perhaps
to want to perpetuate it even to the extent of
making work for it. Well, here we have then
our wonderful company of visitors full of real
care for the people, with time and intelligence
to apply the wisest principles, did they but
know them, with fullest thought, to individual
cases; capable of inspiring confidence, of win-
ning allegiance; of getting those whom they
visit to understand what is best for their future,
and to make up their minds to do it. Is not
this precisely what is needed—the individual
thought which can apply the wise principles,
the love which can influence the wills which
should be brought into harmony with those
principles? Then turn to consider how these
principles are now being thought out, with
what painstaking devotion, what science, what
accuracy some of our greatest men are studying
them. What a mass of information they have
accumulated! How day by day they are
learning to explain better the meaning of it

all ! Think of the doctors, the legislators, the poor-law reformers, the advocates of co-operation, the members of the Charity Organisation Society, how they examine, study, and expound. Once duty to the poor was supposed to consist in giving large alms ; once, self-sacrifice and devotion were thought sufficient qualifications for a worker among the poor ; now it is seen that to these must be added the farthest sight, the wisest thought, the most self-restraining resolution to make a useful worker.

These two classes, gentle doers and wise thinkers, stand far apart, yet, if they could be brought into close communication, both would gain much ; the people for whom they are both labouring would gain much more.   In what follows I have tried to show how such a communication might be made a practical reality. The scheme described is not based wholly on theory, but has substantially been in operation in a district of Marylebone for some years, and has been lately adopted by two other districts.

To effect a union, to establish communication with so numerous a body as the district visitors of London, would be in itself difficult. The difficulty is increased by the fact that they are not only a very numerous, but very changeful body ; not only does death, marriage, or migration take them wholly away, but they are often interrupted by temporary absence from home, household duties, illness, and this far more than would be the case with paid workers, their district work being only a secondary, though a very real, duty. These incessant changes could never, without enormous labour and much likelihood of confusion, be registered at one centre ; and this necessitates that the visitors must be dealt with by certain selected persons, who may be local leaders or centres. Large numbers of them are already gathered in district groups, round various churches and chapels. My first very natural thought was to ask the ministers of those churches and chapels to accept new duties towards their visitors, to bring before them whatever it might seem to the theorists ought to come under their notice, and to transmit to the theorists any individual problems quite too hard for solution in the locality, and to be ready to furnish other information to visitors on questions affecting the temporal condition of their people.   But it was obviously impossible to ask hard-worked London clergymen and ministers to undertake additional work, especially such a work as this.   For its whole value should depend on the constant, living, detailed interchange of information.   And, besides, though the district visitors attached to churches and chapels are by far the most numerous bodies to be enrolled, there are other groups which it is important to secure, and there are also individual visitors to be enlisted who might be ready to help with tangible work, and not prepared to take spiritual work. And this is another reason for not asking the clergy to take up the task.   On the whole,

then, it appears to me best to suggest leaving
the question of all spiritual and moral work
exactly where it is—where it almost must be,
gathering round the clergy and ministers,
everything affecting it being referred to them,
and of course all funds and charities now in
their hands being as hitherto managed and
distributed wholly under their direction; but
at the same time to ask them to consider
whether they could single out someone from
each ecclesiastical district, or from any given
group of visitors, who should be a secretary to
the others—a means of communication between
them and the people dealing as officials or
theorists with questions affecting large bodies
of the poor.

I will describe what I think such a secretary
should be and do.

She need at first have no special knowledge
of laws affecting the poor, institutions established for them, or the principles of action
which those who have thought most on the

subject unite in thinking best ; ladies furnished
with such knowledge would not be found in
many districts, and though such information
would doubtless be of immense value, it would
not be essential to secure it at first, as a great
deal would be rapidly acquired by anyone
holding the post of which I speak.   She ought
to have a good deal of time for writing, and
seeing her fellow-workers.   She need not have
time for visiting the poor.   In fact I should
advise selecting someone who had experience
in visiting them, but was content to resign
that work, as I think her full available power
should be devoted to her secretarial duties.
She should be able, however, to attend regularly at least one meeting weekly of the
Charity Organisation Committee of her district.   If she has a house of her own, or so
much control over one as would enable her
to see the visitors often there, it would be a
great advantage ; in fact, some way of seeing
them frequently and individually appears to

me essential. She should be one who, for the greater part of the year, is resident in town ; for though of course a temporary successor could be appointed, or her post left vacant, absences, especially if frequent, would be a drawback to her usefulness. She ought to have tact, gentleness, and firmness. She must be a careful, conscientious woman of business, with clear head, or very methodical ways; for next to ready sympathy, method will be of all things most necessary to her. Such a secretary should, in that capacity, busy herself only with matters relating to the temporal condition of the poor. She would have relations to her own group of visitors, to the locality in which she lived, and to the metropolis generally. Those to her own fellow-workers would be different probably in different cases ; but I suppose she would help and advise new visitors, tell them of the local charities, consult with them about special cases, register their temporary absence, getting

D

the clergy to fill in such gaps if possible,
show them how to keep written records of
families under their charge in given form, so
as to be of use to succeeding visitors, whether
temporary or permanent, and communicate to
visitors, new and old, all facts within her
knowledge which might be of value to them.
With regard to the local organisation, I will
not stay to describe in detail the ways in
which she might be valuable to the School
Board officer, to the relieving officer, to the
inspector of nuisances, who might learn to
look to her for more radical means of help
than are at their command, both material and
moral, and for information as to details such
as rarely reaches officials, and yet might
enable them to bring beneficent laws more
powerfully to bear on special 'cases. The
secretary should not only avail herself of the
investigating machinery of the Charity Organisation Society, but she should, as I said,
attend the committee meetings. There she

will learn an immense deal about wise principles of relief, new and important facts of law affecting the people, and the working of various institutions; in short, she ought to get there nearly all the instruction she requires. She would also be invaluable to the committee. She would be well acquainted with the principles on which relief is given by those whom she represents, could tell whether they would be likely to make a grant in a certain case, and, approximately, how large such grant would be. She would know, too, how to enlist that individual gentle help which is so often needed in cases coming before the Charity Organisation Society after the preliminary investigation is made, and which the paid agent has neither time nor capacity to give. In fact, for applicants from every street, and court, and lane, in which a visitor was at work, she would know to whom to turn for the personal attention which the Charity Organisation Committee feel they so

urgently need. Nor would her services end
there. Not only would she obtain the aid of
the visitors she represented at such times of
crisis in the history of a poor family as those
in which they usually apply to the Charity
Organisation Society, not only would she be
able to supply a detailed report of the past
life of the applicant on points which might bear
on the committee's decision, but afterwards,
when the decision was made and relief granted
or withheld, through succeeding years she
would get the people watched over with that
continuous care without which right decisions
at any particular crisis of life lose half their
efficacy; indeed, she might often avert such
a crisis altogether. For instance, she might
get the visitors to induce the man to join a
provident dispensary or club; which would be
more satisfactory, though not perhaps more
necessary, than refusing him aid when he has
not done so. Sometimes, when I think of
those Charity Organisation Committees so

much misunderstood by many, because they
have so resolutely determined to give no fresh
unsatisfactory relief, some of them tenderly
pitiful of the poor, some of them a little far
off from them, but all trying to help them in
thoughtfully considered ways, and of the great
current of careless, inconsiderate relief going
on unchecked and uncontrolled by them, I
feel as if a union between you and them would
do more than almost anything else to help
the poor. There they are all ready for you
in every district of London, asking you to
co-operate, asking you to study with them
what is best, and you leave them in too many
cases to be mere repressors of the grossest
forms of mendicity, and by no means organisers
of charity. If the plan I suggest were adopted
by only a few visiting societies, I delight to
think what might be gained by furnishing the
committees with a few gentle workers repre-
senting many more, and associated with the
charities of the neighbourhood.

But I pass on to consider the relations of
these secretaries to the metropolis. They ought
to be supplied with information about the laws
affecting the poor, Sanitary Laws, Poor Laws,
Education Acts, &c.; they ought to get notice
of important meetings about medical charities;
of new suggestions and arrangements as to
the best methods of collecting and storing
the earnings of the poor. And how is this
to be done? Much of it might even now
be done through the Charity Organisation
Society. All of it, I hope, will be done
through the Society in the future; but the
committees are too busy, too occupied with
their daily labour, to deal with this new matter
with the fulness of detail which at first it will
require; and perhaps they do not everywhere
nor always command the full sympathy and
confidence of their district.   Added to which,
I have noticed that people, curiously enough,
are more willing to invite information from
private persons than from official bodies. Some-

thing must be done to meet the wants of a time of transition, and I trust I am not over-bold in offering, while the plan is new, to do what I can to fill the gap; but in the future we ought to endeavour to secure that the visitors should be so organised that they themselves can compare notes, and each communicate to each how practical difficulties have been met in particular localities—so organised that facts bearing on their work should reach them swiftly and certainly, and that their experience should be accessible for legislators and reformers.

I have set before you nothing great, nothing grand, no new society, no fresh light even on the problems respecting wiser systems of relief, or their applications to individuals, which you are desiring so much to solve, each in your own parish or court. I do believe those problems to be capable of solution. I do believe that our almsgiving has been cruel in its kindness. It is for the sake of the people themselves that I would see it decreased, yes, even put down altogether ; I believe they would be richer, as well as happier, for it. For the sake of the energy of the poor, the loss of which is so fatal to them, for the sake of that intercourse with them, happy, friendly, human intercourse, which dependence renders impossible, seek to your utmost for better ways of helping them. We can give you no general rules which will obviate necessity of thought, singly must your difficulties be met, singly conquered; but see that you throw upon them all available light from the experience of others, the thoughts of the thoughtful. No new society, no great scheme, have I to urge, only if here or there any one or two of the groups of visitors care to select one among them to be their secretary, and send me her name and address, I will tell her what I can which I think may be helpful to her or them. We might meet, too, we secretaries, now and again, to talk over important questions and strengthen one another; and though I could not possibly find time to deal with difficulties in detail, I might show, or get shown, what plans have been found useful in places which I know. I might help, too, a little about finding employment. I hear of a good many situations of an exceptional kind, and difficult to fill up suitably, and notice of such vacancies I might send on to secretaries, who could find among their visitors someone who would care to spend thought and time in fitting into an exceptional place the person best adapted for it. The large demands for labour are, I believe, best dealt with by advertisement or registry; but there is not any more valuable way of helping individuals than by fitting them in where they are wanted, in ways that are not possible except to those who have personal knowledge of candidates. Mere routine notices might thus meet great human needs.

I have spoken throughout this paper of outward means and appliances; I have referred very little to improvement of the lives and spirits of men. This is not because I do not care for those lives and spirits. They are reached, we must remember, in many different ways. A great deal of life is necessarily spent in getting its surroundings into order, and in London here, this machinery of ours, all the tangible things round us, need a great deal done to them ; it tests us better than any words can do. It is very difficult—impossible, I believe—to make the things of this world fair and orderly, to arrange them justly, to govern them rightly, without living very nobly. The right use of money, the laws affecting houses and lands, involve principles which test the sincerity of a man or a nation ; they test it, I say, as words cannot test it. I think our poor see this very clearly, and that, strange as it may seem, the messages about God's nature, and about His relation to them, come in a subtle way through our acts. More perhaps than through our words. This is

emphatically so just now. They have heard
a great many words, and have been puzzled
because our actions have often seemed to them
at variance with those words. I know how
hopelessly we must fail in any attempt to live
up to the unspeakable majesty of God's ten-
derness, and the boundless wisdom of His
righteousness; but even our failure, after sincere trial, brings a message of what He is to His
children. Our actions are speaking to them.
For this reason I have never felt the execution
of the most minute duty with regard to tangible
things beneath my notice, and I do not feel
that in urging any of you to consider the
right settlement of questions of temporal relief, I am asking you to devote yourselves to
a task which is otherwise than holy. On the
contrary, I have felt that it can be only rightly
dealt with by those who are content to carry
it on in silent allegiance to One who will
judge with farther sight than feeble men,
who will know what deeper mercy there may

be in the act which looks to men harsh at the moment. Indeed, I dare not trust the difficult things there may be to do in refusal of immediate help to any mere reasonable political economist. The generals who can direct the sad retracing of our foolish steps should be those who care for the people because their Father cares, and so desire to make them what He would have them to be; and the only ones who will have fortitude to bear the misunderstanding this may cause will be those who feel tenderest pity for the people.

Not a small thing, even in itself, is the dealing with the tangible and soulless things of earth. We may be very proud, justly proud, of the well-ordered spot of earth, the well-spent income, the self-restrained providence, whether they are our own, or whether we have helped another so to regulate the talents entrusted to him; but the glad pride breaks away, and a deep thankfulness overpowers us, if ever by word or deed we seem to have helped anyone to catch even a little glimpse of that mighty Love which enwraps his spirit, uniting it in solemn harmony with all that *is* contained, as well as all that *cannot* be contained, in this wonderful, visible world.

III.

A FEW WORDS TO VOLUNTEER VISITORS AMONG THE POOR.*

YOU have asked me to speak to you to-day about work in this parish, and you know I have not the' pleasure of knowing it or you. If anything I say is inapplicable you must forgive my ignorance ; but if I am able to give you any hints which are of use it will not be strange, for one comes across the same kind of difficulties in many various districts of London just now. After the paper is read, if there are any special questions affecting your own district which any of you care to ask me about, I shall be delighted to answer

* Read at Westminster, June 23rd, 1876.

them to the best of my power from this place, or we will have a little general conversation about them later.

Now I am going to say a great deal about hurtful gifts ; but do not misunderstand me, and jump to a conclusion that because I speak of these I have lost sight of the great and good gifts we are each of us bound to make. The needs of the poor we must consider our special charge, and each of us give what we can that *is* real help—not only time, and heart, and spirit, and thought, but money too ; only we must see that it is really helpful, which needs thought and experience, and if we haven't experience we must seek it. There are gifts of money to be made ; there are hard workers recovering from illness to be sent to convalescent homes ; there are orphans to be supported and well educated ; there are pensions to feeble old people who have worked hard, to be given to meet their own savings or compensate for lost savings ; there are children to be placed in industrial schools ; girls to be fitted out for service ; travelling expenses to be paid for people going to better fields of work ; but the decision about even these safer forms of gift requires experience. Give, by all means, abundantly, liberally, regularly, individually, with all enthusiasm, by all manner of means, but oh, give wisely too.

Now to secure this wise relief, I am convinced you will require good investigation, co-operation on the part of your donors, thought and time given by your wisest men. All these are essential, but I am not going to dwell on them just now; the part of your work I am naturally most interested in is your district visiting. I wonder whether you have among you instances of the solitary, inexperienced district visitor, and can feel for her difficulties ? Do you know what I mean ? A lady, well born, highly cultivated, well nurtured, becomes convinced that she has duties to the poor. Perhaps some great personal pain

drives her to seek refuge from it in Christian
service of the poor ; perhaps some family loss
darkens her whole horizon, and opens her eyes
to other forms of sorrow ; perhaps some stir-
ring sermon startles her in the midst of tri-
umphant pleasure, making her feel that she
ought to give some slight offering of time to
the poor ; perhaps weariness of all superficial
glitter of amusement makes her seek for
deeper interests in life.   Be it what it may—
desire to do good, or the urgent request of a
friend, or desire to escape pain, she determines
to volunteer as a district visitor. She is wel-
comed by the clergy, and requested to take
such and such a district—I really think she
has often little more preparation or instruction
than that. She does not start with the desire
of knowing the poor, but of helping them ;
help being in her mind synonymous in such
cases with temporal help. She does not think
of them primarily as *people*, but as *poor* people.
But though her ideas naturally therefore turn

E

to questions of *relief* as if these were her main concerns, she has never studied what has been found to be the effect of different ways of alms-giving, she knows little· about the earnings of the poor, little of their habits and expenses, little about poor-law relief, little about the thousand and one societies for granting various kinds of help, little about the individual donors at work in the neighbour-hood, little about distant fields of labour and demands for workers in them. Now just pause and think of the effect of her actions when she begins—as begin she must by the very fact of her view of her duty—to deal practically with questions of relief; questions which, to say the least, are so difficult to deal with wisely that our most earnest, experienced, and thoughtful men pause in awe before them, advance slowly to practical conclusions, and speak humbly about them after years of study. Ladies would pause before they went in and offered to help a house-surgeon at a hospital

by undertaking a few patients for him, yet
are they not doing something like it when
they don't seek advice in district visiting?
Gradually, after weeks, months, perhaps years
of worse than wasted labour, those who persevere begin to realise the disastrous effect
of their action; hundreds who do not steadily
persevere never even catch a glimpse of it,
and go on blindly scattering gifts to the de-
struction of the recipients. For just pause
and think what these gifts do to them. You
or I go into a wretched room; we see children
dirty and without shoes, a forlorn woman
tells us a story of extreme poverty, how
her husband can find no work. We think
it *can* do no harm to give the children boots
to go to school; we give them, and hear no
more. Perhaps we go to Scotland the following week, and flatter ourselves if we remember
the children that that gift of boots at least
was useful. Yet just think what harm that
may have done. Perhaps the woman was a

drunkard, and pawned the boots at once and drank the money; or perhaps the man was a drunkard neglecting his home, and the needs of it, which should have been the means of recalling him to his duties, he finds partially met by you and me and others; or perhaps the clergy have seen that the poor woman cannot support the children and her husband, who is much too ill to find work, and have felt that if she and they are not to die of starvation they must go into the workhouse, for it is the only means of getting enough for them; charity, not being organised in the district, cannot undertake to do all that is wanted for them, and so had better do nothing. For gifts so given may raise false hopes which you and I, now pleasantly enjoying ourselves, never think of. Because we went in and gave those boots, because others like us gave coal-tickets and soup-tickets last winter, what may not turn up? the poor woman asks herself. That gambling, desperate spirit enters into her heart,

the stake being freedom and home. She plays
high : she wins, or loses. We charitable people
first of all never investigated the case to learn
what it really was, what the character of the
people was, whether the home was worth keeping together, whether with or without club-
money it would cost more than we were ready
or able to give; we raised hopes which it is
a chance whether we fulfil; we met the want
before us without thought; we forgot to consider the influence of that action on the life.
Such gifts are uncertain, insufficient, based on
no knowledge. Let us imagine that in another
case. we give to a man whose income is small;
what is the effect on his character of these
irregular doles? Do they not lead him to
trust to them, to spend up to the last penny
what he earns, and hope for help when work
slackens or altogether fails? Does he try, cost
what it may, to provide for sickness, for times
when trade is dull and employment scarce?
Yet though we have by our gifts encouraged

him in not making the effort to do this, are
we quite sure to be at hand when the need
comes? Are we not most likely to be away?
Trade is slack when London is empty and
district visitors away. Every man's riches
depend on his providence; they do so tenfold
more markedly the nearer poverty he is, yet
we have undermined his providence by uncertain action. Do not our doles encourage him to
keep his big daughter at home, earning a few
pence in the street, where she has what she
calls "freedom," instead of training her for
decent service? I believe our irregular alms
to the occupant of the miserable room, to the
shoeless flower-seller, are tending to keep a
whole class on the very brink of pauperism
who might be taught self-control and foresight
if we would let them learn it. I believe too
that our blanket charities, soup-kitchens, free
dormitories, old endowed charities distributing
inadequate doles, have a great tendency to
keep down the rate of wages of the very

lowest class, partly because they come in like a rate in aid of wages, not so regular as that of the old poor - law, yet still appreciable— partly because they tempt large numbers who might raise themselves to hang on to low callings, and make competition fiercer in them and the chance of absolute want greater. The street-sellers and low class desultory workers usually remain what they are by choice; a little self-control would raise them into the ranks of those who are really wanted, and who have made their way from the brink of pauperism to a securer place, and one where they are under better influences. Above all is this true of the children. A little self-control would enable the daughters of most of these people to rise into the class of domestic servants ; and their sons, instead of remaining street-sellers, would soon learn a trade or go to sea if they cared to do regular work. We are largely helping, by our foolish gifts, to, keep them herded together in crowded, dirty,

badly-built rooms, among scenes of pauperism,
crime, and vice. And we each of us think it
is only the two shillings and sixpence, only
the shilling for this or that perfectly justifiable
object we have given. I have sometimes
wanted to move some widow and her children
to the North, where the children would learn
a trade and support themselves well, where the
woman would find much more work at washing
and charring, and where the family would have
a cottage healthy and spacious, instead of the
one close room. The widow has been a little
fearful of making so important a step. If the
guardians, if the clergy, if, above all, the
visitors, have let the need of work teach its
own natural lesson, that family has removed
and has been happy and independent. I have
now several such well established in 'the North.
But if the various donors have broken in with
their miserable pittances of fixed or desultory
relief, the family, in poverty and uncertainty of
income, have dragged on here in London. In

nearly every case requiring help there is some such step of *self*-help which ought to be taken by the family itself, or some member of it; some girl ought to go to service, some boy to get a place, some member of the family to begin learning a trade, some cheaper lodging to be found. Depend on it, you cannot wisely help a family, you cannot tell whether help at all is needed, till the circumstances and character of each member has been well investigated. Lay this to heart as a fact—I am certain of it. Let it be with any of you who desire to do good a strict rule to yourselves to have the case of every family you want to help thoroughly scrutinised. If you can make up your mind not to give anything pending the receipt of a report, so much the better. But if you can't (I think you soon will), at any rate never give a sixpence without sending for a report on the case; it will guide your future action in that and other instances. It is not much I ask of you. The Charity Orga-

nisation Society in every district in London
will do the work for you free of charge. I
am afraid I cannot yet promise you that it
will always advise you as to efficient treatment; some of the committees could, and all
that could would. But it is even more difficult
to advise as to suitable treatment than to
investigate a case, and it is not easy to find
members for thirty-eight committees yet who
know very much of the subject. But every
Charity Organisation Committee will know *far*
more than inexperienced visitors, and I should
strongly advise all visitors to consult the
Committee about families in their district appa-
rently needing relief.

I hope you will notice that I have dwelt on
the need of restraining yourselves from alms-
giving on the sole ground that such restraint
is the only true mercy to the poor themselves.
I have no desire to protect the purses of the
rich, no hard feeling to the poor. I am thinking continually and only of what is really

kindest to them—kindest in the long run, certainly, but still kindest. I think small doles unkind to them, though they bring a momentary smile to their faces. First of all, I think they make them really poorer. Then I think they degrade them and make them less independent. Thirdly, I think they destroy the possibility of really good relations between you and them. Surely when you go among them you have better things to do for them than to give them half-crowns. You want to know them, to enter into their lives, their thoughts, to let them enter into some of your brightness, to make their lives a little fuller, a little gladder. You who know so much more than they might help them so much at important crises of their lives; you might gladden their homes by bringing them flowers, or, better still, by teaching them to grow plants; you might meet them face to face as friends; you might teach them; you might collect their savings; you might sing for and with them; you might

take them into the parks, or out for quiet days
in the country in small companies, or to your
own or your friends' grounds, or to exhibitions
or picture galleries ; you might teach and refine
and make them cleaner by merely going among
them.   What they would do for you I will not
dwell on, for if the work is begun in the right
spirit you will not be thinking of that ; but I
do believe the poor *have* lessons to teach us
of patience, vigour, and content, which are of
great value to us.   We shall learn them in-
stinctively if we are among them as we ought
to be as friends.   It is this side of your relation to them, that of being their friends, which
has given all the value to your work as district visitors ; it has been because you have
been friends, in as far as you have been friends,
that the relation between you has been happy
and good.   The gift has often darkened this
view of you, and prevented the best among the
poor from wishing to know you ; when it has
absolutely been the expression of friendship,

its evil has been reduced to a great extent.
But the gift you have to make to the poor,
depend upon it, is the greatest of all gifts you
can make—that of yourselves, following in `
your great Master's steps, whose life is the
foundation of all charity. The form of it may
change with the ages, the great law remains,
"Give to him that asketh of thee, and from
him that would borrow of thee turn not thou
away;" but see that thou give him bread, not
a stone—bread, the nourishing thing, that
which wise thought teaches you will be to him
helpful, not what will ruin him body and soul;
else, while obeying the letter of the command,
you will be false to its deep everlasting meaning. My friends, I have lived face to face
with the poor for now some years, and I have
not learned to think gifts of necessaries, such
as a man usually provides for his own family,
helpful to them. I have abstained from such,
and expect those who love the poor and know
them individually will do so more and more

in the time to come. I have sometimes been asked by rich acquaintances when I have said this whether I do not remember the words, "Never turn your face from any poor man." Oh, my friends, what strange perversion of words this seems to me. I may deserve reproach ; I may have forgotten many a poor man, and done as careless a thing as anyone, but I cannot help thinking that to give *oneself* rather than one's *money* to the poor is not exactly turning one's face from him. If I, caring for him and striving for him, do in my inmost heart believe that my money, spent in providing what he might by effort provide for himself, is harmful to him, surely he and I may be friends all the same. Surely I am bound to give him only what I believe to be best. He may not always understand it at the moment, but he will feel it in God's own good time.

IV.

A MORE EXCELLENT WAY OF CHARITY.*

YOU have asked me to speak to you to-night, though I am a stranger to your parish, and know nothing of its special needs or special advantages. Why, then, am I here? I suppose I may safely assume that it is mainly because I represent those who have deep care for the poor, and *also* strong conviction that organisation and mature thought are necessary to any action which shall be really beneficial to them. I fancy your parish, like many another—like most others that have not passed through the stage and answered the problem

* Read at a meeting held in a suburban district in July, 1876.

—is just now questioning itself as to whether investigation, organisation, deliberate and experienced decision, which it feels to be essential if wise relief is to be secured, are, or are not, compatible with gentle and kindly relief; whether charity can be fully of the heart, if it is also of the head. If so, how are you to get the full strength of head and heart. If this is impossible, what in the world you are to do, for you cannot give up either. You ask practically, I fancy, when you invite me here, what I think on these points.

I answer, then, emphatically and decidedly, that my experience confirms me entirely in the belief that charity loses nothing of its lovingness by being entirely wise. Now it cannot be wise without full knowledge of the circumstances of those to be dealt with—hence the necessity of investigation; it cannot come to satisfactory conclusions on those facts unless it employs the help of experienced men—hence the need of a committee for decision; it will not be gracious and gentle, nor fully enter into individual needs, unless it secures the assistance of a good body of visitors. I do not wish to draw your attention to any special form of organisation, but I believe you will find, the more you think of it, that some form is needed, and that whatever it be, it will have to secure those three as essentials—good investigation, decision by a wise committee, and the help of a staff of visitors.

I shall say nothing further on the first head, Investigation, except that I consider it is done best by a good paid officer. A great deal of the preliminary work is quickly and well done by an experienced person, which it would be difficult for a volunteer to do; neither is it a sort of work which it is worth while for a volunteer to undertake. I refer to verifying statements as to residence, earnings, employment, visiting references, and employers. The finishing touches of investigation, the little personal facts, the desires and hopes, and to a certain extent

F

the capacities of the applicant, no doubt a
.volunteer visitor would learn more thoroughly,
but that can always be done separately from
the preliminary and more formal inquiry.

And now to turn to the consideration of
the visitors—those who must be the living
links binding your committee with the poor,
the interpreters of their decision, the bearers
of their alms, the perpetual guardians to prevent renewed falling into want. I have spoken
in so many other places of the extreme value
of such a body working in concert with a
wise committee, and of the mistakes they are
likely to make where undirected, that I am
unwilling to dwell on either point in much
detail here. I will only briefly reiterate that
I think no committee can do its work with
real individual care unless it contains those
who will watch over each family with continuous interest, interpret its decisions intelli-
gently and kindly, and learn all personal detail
which may assist the committee in judging

rightly. Unhappily, visitors have very seldom
any special training for their work, nor is the
need of it pointed out to them. I earnestly
wish we could get this recognised; not that
any should be deterred from working from
want of training, but that in every district
some plans for advising and helping the inexperienced visitors, and binding all visitors
more together, should be adopted. I have,
in a paper read elsewhere, given a sketch
of a practical scheme for securing this end.
But even without the help there spoken of,
visitors might try to look a little farther into
the result of their action. They think of the
immediate effect, and very little of the future
one. Now in all things we must beware of
hasty action. It is not well, in the desire to
alleviate an immediate want, to produce worse
want in the future. I do not know the poor
of your district: there may be many more
of them, and they may be poorer, than I
suppose; but in really populous poor parishes

I have found, and surely you should find here, *that, an immense deal more might be done by the people for themselves than has been done hitherto. Whatever may be the difficulties of finding work for them, aim at that first. Try to get them to bring up their children to callings requiring skill, and which will raise them to the higher ranks of labour; help them to save; encourage them to join clubs; lend them books; teach them to cultivate and care for flowers. These and other like influences will indirectly help them far more even as to outward comforts, than any gifts of necessaries. But do not, when a family wants help, hesitate to give largely, if adequate help will secure permanent good. Remember, if you establish people in life so that they can be self-supporting, it is well worth while to do it, cost what it may.

I know little of your parish. But if it be, as I fancy, one in which the rich are many and the poor few compared to other places,

I should like to add a word or two to such
residents as are in good health and working
here, urging them to consider the needs of
more desolate districts, and pause to think
whether or not they could transfer some of
their time to them. I know it is a difficult
question, and one to be judged in each case
on its merits. I know well what may be
urged on the ground of individual friendships
formed with dwellers in your neighbourhood,
on the score of want of strength and time,
and the claims of your own parish. Weigh
these by all means, but think of the other side
too, if by chance you can realise it. Friendship with poor old women in your district!
Respect its claims; but are there no times
when it may be worth while to make a change
in work, even if it cause one to see less of
friends? Have you ever seen the ward of
an East End workhouse, where from year's
end to year's end the old women live without
any younger life round them, no sons or

daughters whose strength may make their feebleness more bearable, no little grand-children to be cared for, and make the old which is passing forget itself in the young which is coming into vigour! Is your bright young presence not asked for by the gray, monotonous, slowly-ebbing life of those wards? If your strength does not allow you to visit in remote districts, I grant that an unanswerable argument; for strength is meant to be temperately used and not thrown away. Time! Well, it takes time to go backwards and forwards; but isn't one hour where the need is great and the workers very few worth more than many hours in a more favoured district?

Have you ever realised what those acres and acres of crowded, heated, badly-built houses, over which you pass so quickly by train when you go in and out of London, mean? What kind of homes they make? What sort of human beings live and die there? Have you asked yourselves whether your pre-

sence, your companionship, is needed there?
Whether the little children want your teaching? Whether your gentleness, your refinement, your gaiety, your beauty, are wanted
there? Neighbourhood! Oh yes, it has strong
claims—some of the best possible ; but then we
must take care that we let our neighbours
come round us naturally, rich *and* poor. I
only know this neighbourhood as I see it
from the station, and it is possible it is otherwise inside, for I know quarters where the
poor lodge often escape the eye of a casual
observer ; but I do know districts which *are*
very like what yours *looks*, where the villas
cover all the ground, and there is no place
for the poor man's cottage. Where the idea
of building for him would be mentioned with
awed abhorrence by the comfortable residents,
and they would talk about the unpleasantness
of the poor living so near, chances of infection,
&c. &c. Where the few persons required to
serve the needs of the residents live, in a some-

what pampered and very respectful dependence, in small districts decently withdrawn from view, visited and over-visited by ladies who haven't far to go—where the poor say there isn't a house to be had, and the rich say they get everything from a distance.

While you are determined to have the *rich* neighbourhoods, you must have the poor ones elsewhere. When you have gathered the poor round you, built for them, taught them, purified their houses and habits by your near presence, by all means talk about the claims of neighbourhood. But till then you must, I believe, take a wider outlook, and think of the neighbourhoods you have left, where moreover those who indirectly serve you earn their bread. You who are merchants' wives and daughters, nay, even those of you who buy the merchants' goods, have the dock-labourers no claims upon you? If the question, Who is my neighbour? is asked by you, how do you think God answers it from heaven when He looks down

and sees the vast multitudes of undisciplined
poor by whose labour you live, and the few
heroic workers whose lives are being spent
for those poor almost forsaken by you ?

And if some of you went there to give what
little of leisure, what little of strength, you
have to spare, would your own neighbourhood
suffer ? I fancy not. For it seems as if usually
where there are few poor and many rich living
near together, the former become dependent
in fat unenergetic comfort on the latter ; and
if this be such a neighbourhood, a few finding
a call for their sympathy and help elsewhere
might do good to all. It might be a real
blessing to the place where you live to transfer
to other and needier districts some of the
superfluous wealth and unneeded care which
from its very abundance may be spoiling and
pampering your native poor. What a good
thing it might be if each of your congregation
here would undertake to help with money
and with workers some poor district where

wise principles were being strenuously and faithfully worked out. Only remember, though you may send your money, and send it to those who use it wisely, the gift is a very poor one compared with that of yourselves. It is *you* who are wanted there, your love, your knowledge, your sympathy, your resolution—above all, your knowledge; for if you saw, you could not leave things as they are. For instance, on a summer evening sultry as this, there are thousands of families who have no place to sit in but one close room, in which the whole family has eaten, slept, washed, cooked. It is stifling. They go to the doorstep; their neighbours are at their steps. It gets hotter, the children swarm in the narrow court; the dust flies everywhere; the heat, the thirst is insufferable, the noise deafening, the crowd bewildering; they go to the public-house: do you wonder? It may be there are a few spaces unbuilt over close by, but who will open the gates for them, plant a few flowers, put a few seats ? The garden of Lincoln's Inn Fields is certainly kept very lovely; but how few eyes are allowed to see it; Red Lion Square is a howling ugliness; the Board School playgrounds are closed on Saturday;* the little graveyard in Drury Lane†—half the graveyards in London—are close locked and barred, and left in ugliness too; the Quakers are actually deciding to sell for building purposes their ancient burial-ground near Bunhill Fields.‡ Can they not afford to let the place allotted to their dead be consecrated to the poor and become a place of rest to the weary living before their pilgrimage is over ? Money, money, money, to spend where we see its effect in parks, or villas, or cosy suburban houses, and not a glimpse of what we might do with it in the districts where the poor live and die.

* Eighteen of these are now to be opened.
† Now open to the public, and planted as a garden.
‡ Since sold for building.

Of course this is only one side of the truth, and no one knows the converse better than I. I know how people are coming forward year by year to do and to feel more and more of their duty to the poor. The interest deepens and spreads, and that rapidly. Haven't I myself such a body of fellow-workers as makes me hardly know how to be thankful enough? And doubtless many of you here are doing exactly what I urge, or better things than I have thought of. But forgive me if the sight of all that is needed sometimes makes me a little impatient, and urge the point with some implied reproach towards those who delay to come and do what it looks as if they might. I daresay they may many of them have better reasons than I know for holding aloof: all have not the same duties; but sure I am that the need is urgent, and that to many such work would add new and deeper interests to life. I only say, " Look for yourselves what the need is, consider what your duty may be, and when seen do it resolutely, quietly, hopefully."

And now, leaving the subject of visitors, let us consider, in conclusion, the third point essential to wise dealing with the poor—the decisions of your committee after the facts are gathered for it by investigating agent and volunteer visitor. Now, to secure right decision, one must have a distinct object in view. What is to be the ultimate object of your decisions respecting relief? Let us at once distinctly clear the way by assuming that it must be the good of the people themselves. We have nothing to do with saving the money of the rich. It is possible—nay, probable—that in our first attempts to put charity on a right footing, we may have to spend more than we did before, and make larger demands on the purses of the wealthy. A few substantial gifts, wisely bestowed, may easily make up a larger sum than a multitude of petty careless doles. A weekly pension, a grant of a few pounds to help a family to migrate, is more than the money-equivalent of many a random shilling. But if, on reflection, we decide to withhold gifts of any kind whatsoever, it is only to be done for the sake of the people themselves. If doles, or bread-tickets, or coal-tickets, are proved to help the people, we are bound to give them to the extent of our power. If they are proved to injure them, we are bound not to give them, however pleasant it may be, however easy, however it may seem to pave the way for other influences. Do we want to make the poor depend on relief, which is ready at a moment's notice, instead of having the fortitude to save a little to meet a sudden emergency? If so, we shall be always treating cases as urgent, and relieving pending investigation, and assuming that discretionary power of granting instant help must be vested somewhere besides in the relieving-officer. I know parishes where benevolent people plead that starvation or great need may arise if they have a weekly committee and no officer empowered to deal with urgent cases. Suppose we ourselves had lost the pride of independence which does still exist in the middle and upper classes, though the tendency to look for extraneous help is, I sometimes fear, eating gradually upwards; but suppose we had no hesitation on the score of pride in asking our richer neighbour for a meal, or new clothes or boots, or additional blankets, or a ton of coal, would it be better for us to use just the amount of providence necessary for us to go to him a week beforehand and say, " Please we shall want our dinner next Sunday," or would it be better for us to be led to expect that if we called on Saturday to tell him the fact, and he was out at a garden-party, when he came home he would say: " Dear me, perhaps they have no dinner, and Sunday too. I dare not wait to see why they are in want; whether there is any member of the family who might be helped to a place where he can earn more. I'd better send some roast meat. I don't like to be enjoying myself at garden-parties with my wife and daughter and not consider my poorer neighbours"? Do you think that, be our earnings much or little, that kind of help would be likely to be helpful? The smaller the earnings the more need of providence; and there is no man so poor but he might, by effort, at least have a few shillings in hand for emergency, if he really felt it important. Literally, that is all that is wanted to do away with this clamour about urgency. That every man should at some time of his life put aside five or ten shillings which should be ready for need, and apply for help directly he saw need to draw upon that, instead of when he hadn't a crust in the house. I don't know whether you are troubled with this great bugbear of "urgency" here; it frightens many districts, but always disappears when approached. Depend upon it, starvation cases are more likely to arise where we have trained our poor to look for instantaneous help, than where they rely on their own forethought at least to the extent I have mentioned ; for *if* they trust to sudden aid, and any accident prevents their receiving it, then they have no money, and are in need indeed. Depend on it, the poor-law, which the poor do not turn to readily, which has, moreover, a strong permanent machinery in every parish in England, is the only right source of relief for urgent cases. No respectable family but has friends, neighbours, or savings to fall back on just while you look well into their cases. Those who are not respectable want, and, in my estimation, should have, help ; but they cannot be helped easily with grants in urgent haste ; they need thought, and influence, and much power. If, then, we decide that urgent cases can be left to the poor-law, your committees will have those only left to deal with whose circumstances they can

G

thoroughly know and deliberately decide upon. And these, I believe they will find, class themselves into cases in which temporary help will raise the applicants into permanently self-supporting positions, and chronic cases. The first, no doubt, they will try to help liberally, carefully, and kindly. The second they will probably help only if they can do so adequately, which I should fancy here you might easily do, if you all heartily and thoughtfully co-operated, and knew each what the other was doing, so that no work was done twice over. Such organisation of alms-giving would be, I should think, the limit of your aim at present.

Perhaps you will also add to these relieved persons a very large number of sick, whom I should be glad to see after, say, a year's notice, forced into some independent form of sick-club.

For I do not myself believe that we from above can help the people so thoroughly and well in any other way as by helping them to help themselves. This I think they are meant to do—this I believe they can do by association and by forethought. When they do provide necessaries for their own families, I think it leaves our relation to them far better, and enables us to help them more fully in better ways. After all, what are the gifts of these outside things compared to the great gifts of friendship, of teaching, of companionship, of advice, of spiritual help ? I know some people think the half-crown, or packet of tea, the best introduction to these. I cannot say I have seen it so. I do not remember a single example in any age or country in which a class in receipt of small occasional doles was in a position of honourable healthy friendship with the givers of such, or fit to receive from them any intelligent teaching. Of course the receipt of alms produces curtsies and respectful welcomes, and perhaps attendances at church or chapel from those who care more for the

G 2

gifts than for the quiet dignity of independence
which is found in many humble people ; more
for the good tea.than for any sermon or service.
But how do the better ones feel it ? Haven't
your gifts absolutely tended to alienate them
from churches and chapels ? Do they not
scorn them, and desire to be seen to benefit
nothing by them ? The application for help
is nearly always made by the wife, and the
respectable husband would no more make it
than you or I would, in nine cases out of ten.
Only notice what happens whenever the rule
is that the man must come up to ask for help ;
they hardly ever come, but simply earn the
needed amount. And among the women, too,
the better ones hold aloof from anything that
looks like bribery to come to a place of
worship. I would ask any clergyman whether
he does not think that the mixing of temporal
gifts with spiritual teaching has not a direct
tendency to lower the value of the teaching
in the eyes of the recipient ? Of old, when

apostles preached, they treated the Gospel as good news which the people would care to receive for itself; they honoured it in treating it as if it were a blessing. Of course it is difficult to distinguish between the actions which come from the radiant outpouring of every species of good gift in mere wealth of joyful human love springing from vivid sense of Divine love, which we see in earnest preachers of all ages, from the gift which is meant to be, and felt to be, a bribe. In many cases, probably, the gifts comprise a mixture of love and a purpose to attract, which it would be impossible to separate. But religious teaching, I have no manner of doubt whatever, has suffered of late years incomparably more than it has gained by this confusion. Let the gift, then, stand or fall by its own intrinsic value; if it be helpful in itself, cultivating such right qualities as will make the recipient richer in such outside things as itself, let it be made. If not, withhold it. And for God's sake let

His truth stand on its own merits. If it be a real need of His children, trust Him in His own good time to make this plain to them. Preach it by word, by deed, by patient abiding ; but do not use bribes, or even what look like bribes, to make men take it in. Depend on it, it cannot be taken so. It has been accepted in this and other ages by men ready to meet poverty, toil, scorn, death, rather than be false to it ; it has been accepted with acclaim by multitudes who felt in it the answer to their difficulties, the great good news for their lives. The lowest natures, when they have received it, have done so through the noble feelings which are latent in the worst of us. It is only through appeal to these—their fortitude, their reverence—that it can come home to them. I cannot believe that God's truth has ever entered one human heart wrapped up in a bribe. Let it speak quietly for itself; it is very strong. Shall we doubt it ? Our special form of it, or application

of it, may not commend itself to our neighbours. Do not let this disappoint us ; let us
with single-minded zeal try to get those neighbours to be and to do what they see to be
right, and then will be revealed to them,
gradually, whatever form of truth they can
comprehend and apply. They will help to
form God's Church, which is of many members ;
and if

> Our little systems have their day,
> They have their day and cease to be,

we must remember that the words go on :

> They are but broken lights of Thee,
> And Thou, O Lord, art more than they.

V.

A WORD ON GOOD CITIZENSHIP.

I HAVE often, on previous occasions, felt bound to urge, not only the evils of indiscriminate alms-giving, but the duty of withholding all such gifts as the rich have been accustomed to give to the poor. At the same time I have realised so fully how tremendous the responsibility of abstaining from such gifts is considered by the donors, that I have not thought they could act on my advice without themselves seeing that it would be merciful as well as wise to withhold such gifts. I have, therefore, usually said : " Look for yourself, but look with the sound of my words ringing in your ears." And those words have been distinctly to proclaim that I myself have no belief whatever in the poor being one atom richer or better for the alms that reach them, that they are very distinctly worse, that I give literally no such alms myself, and should have no fear for the poor whatever if any number of people resolved to abstain from such alms. But, on the other hand, I have long felt, and feel increasingly, that it is most important to dwell on the converse of the truth.

The old forms in which charity expressed itself are past or passing away. With these forms are we to let charity itself pass? Are there no eternal laws binding us to charitable spirit and deed? 'Are we, who have become convinced that doles of soup, and loans of blankets, and scrubbing-brushes sold at less than cost-price, have failed to enrich any class —have helped to eat out their energy and self-reliance — thereon to tighten our purse-strings, devise new amusements for ourselves, expend more in luxurious houses and expensive dinners, cultivate our own intellects, indulge elegant tastes, and float down the stream of Time in happy satisfaction that the poor cannot be bettered by our gifts—in fact, must learn self-help—we meantime going to flower-shows, or picture galleries, or studying systems of political economy? Are the old words, " Bear ye one another's burdens," to pass away with the day of coal-tickets?   Have the words, " Ye are members one of another," ceased to be true because our tract and dole distribution has broken down ? Are there no voices still speaking in our hearts the old commandment, " Love one another ? "   Is that love to be limited henceforward to the pleasant acquaintances who call upon us, and like the same poets, and can talk about Rome and the last clever book ? Or is it, as of old, to go forth and gather in the feeble, the out-of-the-way, the poor ?   Is humanity, is nationality, is citizenship too large for our modern love or

charity to embrace, and shall it in the future
be limited to our family, our successful equals,
or our superiors? Are we going to look out
and up, but never down? The love of our
Master Christ, the love of St. Francis, the love
of Howard, the love of John Brown, the
burning love of all who have desired to serve
others, has been a mighty, all-embracing one,
and specially tender, specially pitiful. All
modern forms of alms-giving may pass and
change, but this love must endure while the
world lasts. And if it endure, it must find
expression. Charity such as this *does* find
expression. It finds expression, when healthiest
and most vigorous, not in weak words, but in
strong acts. If we would not be mere butter-
flies and perish with our empty, fleeting, self-
contained lives; if we would not be fiends of
intellectual self-satisfaction living a cold and
desolate life; if we would not leave the hungry,
the forlorn, the feeble, to perish from before us,
or to rise and rend us; we must secure such

love as that which lighted and intensified the lives of heroes and of missionaries, and struggle to see what scope there is for acts which shall embody that love.

The mistake the old-fashioned donors make is not in their benevolence — that cannot be too strong—but they forget to watch whether the influence of their deeds is beneficent. I should not at all wonder if even thirty years ago doles were more beneficent than now. If the poor had at that time not learned to trust to them, if they came straight from the loving hands of those who cared to step aside from beaten tracks to know and serve the poor they must have had very different results from any they have now, when people *have* learned to depend on them, when they are almost the fashion, and often the relief for the consciences of those who don't feel quite easy, if they give *no* time, *no* heart, *no* trouble, nor *any* money to the poor. I have no manner of doubt, that just now gifts of necessaries are injurious.

What form, then, shall our charity take in the immediate future?

Take that question home to yourselves, each of you who has not answered it already; ask it of yourselves, not as if you were asked to take the position of hero, or martyr, or professed philanthropist, but as if I had said to you, "What do you, as a man or woman, feel bound to do beyond the circle of your family for those who are fellow-men, fellow-citizens, many of them sunk into deep ruts of desolation, poverty, and sin?" Find some answer, live up to it, so shall your own life, your own city, your own age be better.

I will tell you what kind of answer I think may come to you. First, as to money, which is perhaps the most difficult thing to give without doing harm. Don't sit down under the conviction that therefore you are to buy or spend it all for yourself. If you like to earn rather less, to pause in middle life, and give full thought to spending what you have,

or, better still, to give time which might have
made money, I shall certainly not complain
of you.   But do not think there is no scope
for beneficent gifts of money because soup-
kitchens and free dormitories are not beneficent.
There is abundant scope for large gifts, large
enough to please the proudest of you.   Are
there no great gifts of open spaces to be made
for the rich and poor to share alike in the time
to come—spaces which shall be to the child
no more corrupting than the mountain to the
Highlander, or the long sea horizon to the
fisherman's lad ?   They will come to him as
an inheritance he possesses as a Londoner or
an English child ; most likely being taken,
like light and air, straight from God, and not
in any way tending to remind him of men's
gifts, still less to pauperise him.   But if a
memory of you as a donor comes to him as
youth ripens into manhood, long after you are
in your grave, the thought is more likely to
incite him to make some great, abidingly useful

gift to his town, than in any way to paralyse
his energies or weaken his self-respect. Are
there no places to plant with trees, no buildings
to erect, no libraries to found, no scholarships
to endow ? Are there, moreover, none of those
many works to achieve, which a nation, a
municipality, a vestry, first needs to see done,
to learn the use of by using, though finally
such a community may prize them more by
making an effort to establish similar ones ?
For instance, no one would dwell more urgently
than I on the need of making healthy houses
for the poor remunerative ; and now the problem of doing so has been in a great measure
solved. But do we not owe this to the efforts
of a body of men in earlier time who were
content to lose money in experiments and
example ? Pioneers must risk, if not give,
largely, that we may travel smoothly over the
road which they made with such difficulty.
Are we in turn never to be pioneers ? Are
there no improved public-houses, no improved

theatres, no better machinery for collecting savings, which we may establish and give our money to ? The same kind of far-sighted policy might be adopted with all smaller gifts, making them either radically beneficial in themselves, as when they train an orphan for service-work in life, or give rest to an invalid whose savings are exhausted ; or they may be gifts of things which no one is bound to provide for himself, but which give joy—as if you helped to put coloured decoration outside our schools or houses in dingy streets, or invited a company of poor people whom you know to tea in your garden during the fair June weather, or even sent some shells from your home by the sea to small children in one of our few London playgrounds.

But to leave the question of money and come to the greater gift of *time.* Here especially I would beg you to consider whether you have each of you done your utmost. A poor district in London is inhabited by a number of persons, ill-educated, dirty, quarrel-some, drunken, improvident, unrefined, possibly dishonest, possibly vicious. I will assume that we, too, have each of us a good many faults—perhaps we are selfish, perhaps we are indolent. I am sure all the virtue is not among the rich; but certain advantages they surely have which the poor have not—education, power of thinking out the result of certain courses of action, more extended knowledge of facts or means of acquiring it, habits of self-control, habits of cleanliness, habits of temperance, rather more providence usually, much more refinement, nearly always a higher standard, perhaps a high standard, of honesty. Have we not a most distinct place among the poor, if this be so? Is not our very presence a help to them? I have known courts nearly purified from very gross forms of evil merely by the constant presence of those who abhorred them. I know, you probably all know, that dirt disappears gradually in places that cleanly people go in

and out of frequently. Mere intercourse between rich and poor, if we can secure it without
corrupting gifts, would civilise the poor more
than anything. See, .then, that you do not
put your lives so far from those great companies of the poor which stretch for acres in
the south and east of London, that you fail to
hear each other speak. See that you do not
count your work among them by tangible
result, but believe that healthy human intercourse with them will be helpful to you and
them. Seek to visit and help in parishes in
which this is recognised as an end, in itself.

Again, we have got our population into a
state of semi-pauperism, from which individuals
and societies cannot raise them merely by
abstaining from gifts by guardians or with-
drawing out-relief. We have accustomed them
to trust to external help, and only by most
patient individual care shall we raise them.
Neither can we persuade donors, unaccustomed
to study the future results of their acts, to

abstain from distinctly unwise charity unless
we are among them, unless we are ready, too,
to consider with them about each human soul,
which is to them and to us inexpressibly
precious, what is at the moment the wise thing
to do. Have most gentlemen any idea how
much this work needs doing in the poor
districts of London? The Charity Organisation Society came forward now some years ago
to try to get the donors of London to meet
and consider this question in detail in every
district in London. It undertook to look carefully into all cases brought to its offices, and
to report the results of its inquiries. It did *not*
undertake to make additional gifts except where
they might secure enduring benefit, but it said
to the donors, "Associate yourselves, relieve
after due thought, after investigation, and in
conjunction one with another." That Society
has made great way; it has established offices
in every district, and has provided an investigating machinery of inexpressible value, of

H 2

which every Londoner may avail himself. But,
I ask, where are the donors? Where are the
representatives of the various relieving agencies?
The clergy? The district visitors? There are
of course a certain number who have co-
operated heartily, but, as a rule, I am forced
to reply very mournfully, after all these years
they are for the most part going on with their
ill-considered relief very much the same, not
using the machinery, and reproaching the
Charity Organisation Society that *it* is not
relieving largely, and that it is not com-
posed of themselves! Now, till these relieving
agencies come in and take their share, and
give their gentler tone to the somewhat dry
machinery, are these offices to be places where
mere routine business is done by an agent
who cannot have much individual care for the
applicants? Or is there to be anyone to
watch over each applicant with real charity,
questioning him gently, thinking for him sym-
pathetically, seeking for him such help as will

be really helpful? In some offices in the poor districts we have found honorary secretaries to do this, and splendid work it has been. Wherever such help has been forthcoming the poor have been well served, and the old-fashioned donors have been in some measure won to wiser courses of action. But many more such honorary secretaries are needed, and that imperatively and immediately. Are there no men of leisure, with intellect and heart, who will come forward? I have known no such urgent need as this in the many years I have spent face to face with the poor since I came to London—the need of advice, of sympathy, of thoughtful decision for poor man after poor man, as he comes up to our offices at a crisis in his life.

One more instance of the way help can be given, and I have done; for I will not dwell now on the good that might be done by the purchase and management of the houses of the poor, by teaching, by entertainments for

them, by oratorios, by excursions, by the gift
of beautiful things. I will only point out now
that as guardians or vestrymen the most influential sphere of work presents itself. If
you try to get into Parliament, many men of
equal education, high principles, and refinement
probably contest the place with you; if you
succeed they fail; if you try to make a name
among the fashionable or wealthy circles, you
may or may not succeed; but if you fail no
one misses you much. But if, instead of trying
to get high up, you were to try to get down
low, what a position of usefulness you would
have! You would learn much from vigorous
colleagues, much I fancy which would make
you ashamed; but what might not they gain,
what might not the locality gain, if the administration of its affairs were carried on under
the influence of men of education! As guardians, how you might see to the poor, leading
them back to independence in most thoughtful
ways, watching over them individually that no

wrong was done! As vestrymen, how you
might be on the side of far-sighted expenditure or the suppression of corruption! When
I see people all struggling to get up higher,
they seem to me like people in a siege, who
should all rush to defend the breach for the
glory and renown of it, and trample one another
to death, and leave little doors unwatched all
round the town; and I can't help wondering
sometimes why more of them don't pray
Marion Erle's prayer when she leaves the
wedding-dress unfinished to go and nurse the
fever-stricken patient, "Let others miss me,
never miss me, God."

I don't the least mean that the works I have
suggested are the only ones, or the best, or
even that always that *kind* of work may be
best. The form that charity takes in this age
or in that must be decided by the requirements
of the time, and these I describe may be as
transient as others. Only never let us excuse
ourselves from seeking the best form in the

indolent belief that no good form is possible, and things are better left alone ; nor, on the other hand, weakly plead that what we do is *benevolent.* We must ascertain that it is really *beneficent* too.

VI.

OPEN SPACES.*

ALL that is strictly practical that I have to
say to-day could be summed up in a very
few words. I have no changes in the law to
suggest. I have not thought it well to relate
the past history of inclosures, nor even to
prepare for you statistics, neither have I
touched on recent legislation respecting commons. I have had but one end in view in
writing this paper—the laying out and opening small central spaces as public gardens.

I have to interest you in accomplishing
the object. " There is little to see, and little
to say ; it is only to do it," as was once said
by a hard worker. I cannot transport you

*Read at a meeting of the National Health Society, May 9, 1877.

all to see the good sample-work which there
is in some few neighbourhoods in London.
I can, therefore, only ask you to let me
describe in some detail the need of these
gardens, then what has been, and what, it
seems to me, should be, done, with various
kinds of small spaces. This paper contains
this description and information, as to the
very simple preliminary steps necessary to be
taken to render some of these spaces available for public use ; but though so much of
it is thus necessarily descriptive, it is only
on the ground of its bearing on distinct practical results that I trouble you with it.

There are two great wants in the life of
the poor of our large towns, which ought to
be realised more than they are—the want of
space, and the want of beauty. It is true
that we have begun to see that a whole
family living in one room is very crowded,
and we have been for some years well aware
that it would be a good thing if we could

manage so to build that a working man could pay for two or even three rooms; it is true that we have learned that the extreme narrowness of our courts and alleys, and the tiny spaces, often only four or five feet square, called by courtesy "yards," which are to be found at the back of many of the houses filled with families of the poor, appear to us insufficient. We wish we could enlarge them, we wish that Building Acts had prevented landlords thus covering with rent-producing rooms the gardens or larger yards which once existed at the back of high houses; and we are alive to the duty of trying to obviate, as soon as may be, this want of space, to any degree to which it may yet be possible. But there is a way in which some compensation for this evil may be provided, which appears only to have begun lately to dawn upon the perception of men. I mean the provision of small open spaces, planted and made pretty, quite near the homes of the people, which might be used by them in common as sitting-rooms in summer. Even in England there are a good many days when at some hours sitting out of doors is refreshing, and when very hot days do come, it seems almost a necessity.

I fancy very few of you know what a narrow court near Drury Lane or Clerkenwell is on a sultry August evening. The stifling heat, the dust lying thick everywhere, the smell of everything in the dirty rooms, the baking, dry glare of the sun on the west window of the low attic, just under the roof, making it seem intolerable—like an oven. The father of the family which lives there, you may be pretty sure, is round the corner at the public-house, trying to quench his thirst with liquor which only increases it; the mother is either lolling out of the window, screaming to the fighting women below, in the court, or sitting, dirty and dishevelled, her elbow on her knee, her chin on her hand, on the dusty, low door-step, side by side with a drunken woman who comments with foul oaths on all who pass. The children, how they swarm ! The ground seems alive with them, from the neglected youngest crawling on the hot stones, clawing among the shavings, and potato-peelings, and cabbage-leaves strewn about, to the big boy and girl "larking" in vulgarest play by the corner. The sun does not penetrate with any purifying beams to the lower stories of the houses, but beats on their roofs, heating them like ovens. The close staircase is sultry, the dust-bins reek, the drains smell, all the dirty bedding smells, the people's clothes smell. The wild cries of the thirsty, heated, irritated crowd driven to drink, the quarrelling children's voices echo under the low and narrow archway by which you enter the court. Everyone seems in everyone else's way. You begin to wonder whether a human being, man, woman, or child, is in very deed in any sense precious, either to God who made them, or to their

own family, or to their fellow-citizens. Somehow you wonder whether, when one of them
is carried out by the undertaker at last, to
use a common old saying, "His room is not
worth more than his company," so fearful is
the life to which people take under such con-
ditions, so terribly does the need of a little
more space strike you, so impossible seems
any quiet in which tone might be recovered
by these exhausted creatures. And yet every
one of those living beings, crowding almost
under your feet, having to move from door-
way or stair as you enter, has a human form,
a human character too; somebody knows and
loves him, some mother, father, sister, brother,
child, watches for that face among the many,
and would feel a great gap left in the world
if that one came never any more up the
court. Even the reeling drunkard would be
missed. Each is surrounded by a love which
makes him precious, each has also some germ
and gleam of good in him, something you can

touch, or lead, or strengthen, by which in time he might become the man he was meant to be. Each is a child of God, meant by him for some good thing. Put him in a new colony with wood, or heath, or prairie round him, or even lead him into the quiet of your own study, and you will begin to see what is in the man. It is this dreadful crowding of him with hundreds more, this hustling, jostling, restless, struggling, noisy, tearing existence, which makes him seem to himself or you so useless, which makes him be so little what he might be. Can you give him a little pause, a little more room, especially this sultry summer afternoon ?

I think you may. There are, all over London, little spots unbuilt over, still strangely preserved among the sea of houses—our grave-yards. They are capable of being made into beautiful out-door sitting-rooms. They should be planted with trees, creepers should be trained up their walls, seats should be placed

in them, fountains might be fixed there, the
brightest flowers set there, possibly in some
cases birds in cages might be kept to delight
the children.   To these the neighbouring poor
should be admitted free, under whatever regulations should seem best.   The regulations
will vary according to the size of the ground
and other local circumstances.   In some cases
where the ground is large it might, no doubt,
be thrown absolutely open, as Leicester Square
is, a man being always in attendance to keep
order, though the people will themselves help
to keep order very soon.   In the case of very
small grounds admission might be given to
certain numbers by tickets placed in the
hands of guardians, schoolmasters, ministers of
all denominations, Bible-women, and district
visitors.   Though, no doubt, much supervision
would be needed at first, after a time an old
man, any not too feeble old pensioner,
especially if fortified with some kind of
uniform, would be amply sufficient, if always

there, to keep order. His wages would be small, and employing him would be a double charity. In these gardens, near to their own homes, and therefore easily accessible to the old and feeble, they might sit quietly under trees ; there the tiny children might play on gravel or grass, with a sense of Mother Earth beneath them. There comrades might meet and talk, whose homes are too small and wretched for them to sit there in comfort, and for whom the public-house is too often the only place to meet in, or to read the news-paper. If visitors could gather small groups of children together, and use these out-door sitting-rooms as places to teach them games, read to them, or get leave for them to train the creepers up the wall, much good might be done, and much of the evil of playing in the streets prevented.

It is to the conversion of these churchyards into gardens that I would specially turn your attention to-day ; there are a vast number of

I

them all over London, as shown in a map prepared by the Commons Preservation Society,
1, Great College Street, Westminster.

I have ventured to draw the attention of
some few London vicars to the question, and
if you would each of you look in any crowded
neighbourhood known to you, what might be
done, and bring the question before the in-
cumbents, churchwardens, or leading vestrymen,
a great many of these graveyards might rapidly
be made available. Of course there may be
special local difficulties here and there, but
the process is very simple where there is no
opposition; and if those parishes where there
is none would lead the way, that would soon
bring the others to follow so good an example.
The first step to be taken is to secure the
leave of the incumbent of the parish. Notice
must then be placed on the church-doors giving
notice that a vestry meeting will be called to
consider the scheme. The vestry then obtains
a faculty from the Dean of Arches. The

vestry can then be asked for a grant, and they can apply to the Metropolitan Board of Works for a further grant. In the case of St. George's-in-the-East £1,200 was voted by the vestry, and £3,000 by the Metropolitan Board of Works. This was of course a specially expensive scheme, the churchyard itself being large, and the freehold of adjoining ground, which was formerly a burial-ground belonging to dissenters, having to be absolutely bought. The expense in the case of the Drury Lane ground was about £160 ; the vestry became responsible for the whole, but hope the neighbouring parishes and private persons will help. It appears to me that the vestries should in the first instance be applied to, though doubtless private people would gladly help if necessary.

It may be interesting to you to know, so far as I can tell you, what has already been done in planting and opening churchyards. Mr. Harry Jones has induced his vestry to

I 2

co-operate with him, and has made a public
garden of the churchyard of St. George's-in-the-
East. He obtained the hearty co-operation of
his parishioners, and the place bears the stamp
of being one in which they feel they all have
a share. I believe the churchwarden gave the
fountain, and the vestry, instead of having to
be urged on to spend more, actually ordered
24,000 bulbs this spring, in their enthusiasm
to make the place bright and pretty! The
high wall covered with spikes, which separated
the church from the dissenting burial-ground,
has been pulled down, and the whole thrown
into one. The ground has been laid out with
grass, flower-beds, broad gravel walks, and
plenty of seats have been placed there. The
day I was last there, there were many people
in the garden, one or two evidently convales-
cents. The ground was in perfect order, a
gardener and one man being in attendance ;
but the people, though evidently of the lower
class, were clearly impressed with a feeling

that the garden should be respected. In fact the special feature of this garden seemed to me to be the evident sense of its being common property—something that everyone had had a share in doing, and in which they had a common interest. The tombstones are all removed, but measurements were taken, and an authorised plan made of the ground, showing precisely the place of every grave, also a certified copy of every tombstone has been entered in a large book. These precautions for carefully preserving power of identifying the spot where any body is buried, and securing the record of the inscription, have entirely satisfied the owners of graves and the legal authorities, and it would be well for vicars having disused churchyards to remember the plan as one which has met all difficulties in the way of removing tombstones.

The little churchyard in Bishopsgate which has been planted is probably well known to most of you. It is, I believe, a delight to

many. A friend said to me the other day,
"I often pass through it; it is certainly very
nice. The only thing I am sorry about is that
they have taken away the peacock and put
two swans instead." "Are they not as pretty?"
I asked. "Oh, I daresay they are," he replied;
"it was the swans I was thinking of, they
have so small a space, while the peacock was
quite happy, because he always had plenty of
people to admire his tail!" The Rev. G. M.
Humphreys brought the question of opening
the little burial-ground in Drury Lane before
the notice of the St. Martin's-in-the-Fields
vestry. They agreed to carry forward the
work, and it was opened last week to the
people as a garden. It is a refreshing breath-
ing-space in a terribly crowded neighbourhood.
It is bounded by a small piece of ground on
the north which is admirably fitted for a block
of dwellings for working people. If the Duke
of Bedford, to whom I understand it belongs,
would build, or arrange for others to build

there, a block of houses where abundant air
would be secured to them, and transfer there
the population of some crowded court, he would
do a great and good work.

By-the-way, this paper was written before
the news reached me of the temporary closing
of the garden until such time as the vestry
have decided in what way to regulate the admission of the public in future. As much will
doubtless be heard of this temporary closing,
I may as well explain, that my friend, Miss
Cons, was there on Thursday, and saw the
extent of mischief done, and went pretty
thoroughly into the whole question. There
does not appear to have been any destructive-
ness of mischievous feeling—the people availed
themselves in such crowds of the privilege of
going in, that the ivy was very much trampled
on, and the yuccas which had been planted
in the middle of the gravel without any sort
of protection had their leaves spoiled ; but
the shrubs were hardly injured, nor does

there appear to have been any intentional mischief done. It is hardly wonderful that the ivy should be trampled on, seeing that no low wire fence, such as guards the beds in Leicester Square, nor little hoops, such as protect them in St. George's-in-the-East, had been placed. At the same time I may add that, seeing how very small the ground is in proportion to the dense population near Drury Lane, in the letter in which I brought the subject of planting it before the vicar, I suggested opening it by tickets distributed by workers in the district, rather than throwing it absolutely open to everyone. I thought that might have been done later, if it were found possible. I also pointed out to the man in charge, as I left the ground last week, that *at first* much supervision would be needed. If the vestry has the smallest doubt about the possibility of succeeding in keeping it in order, I have not the smallest hesitation in undertaking to do it for them for a year;

if they like to trust me with it, and so meet the first difficulties by special individual care, and prove the possibility of conducting the experiment there, as well as it has been done in St. George's-in-the-East. But I have no doubt they will see their way effectually to carry through the good work they have begun, only I have not had time to communicate with them yet.

The large churchyard in the Waterloo Road is in process of being turned into a garden. The Rev. Arthur Robinson has collected £290, and is laying it out more like a country garden, and less like a place planned by a Board of Works, than any other I have seen. He has stumps prepared for ferns to grow on (and wants some, by-the-way, which some of you might send him); he has a nice bank, winding walks between the turf, knows which side of the church his wisteria will grow, spoke with hope of getting the large blue clematis to flower, wants numberless creepers to cover the church walls, and to wreathe around and make beautiful the few tombs which he leaves unmoved because relatives are still living and care to retain them.   I understand he purposes applying to the vestry for help, and in view of the many churchyards there are to deal with, this would seem the right thing to do in general.   At the same time, I can see we should get a more country-like garden, the more the planning of it could be left in the hands of a man of culture, who loves plants and colour.

I believe St. Pancras Churchyard is now open as a garden ; Limehouse is, I understand, thus utilised as far as the tombstones allow. The Rev. W. Allen has got his parishioners to memorialise the vestry to take some steps towards opening the ground in Bermondsey, but hitherto without success, and there may be others either now laid out or in progress—I earnestly hope there are—of which I have no knowledge.

I regret to say that an attempt to induce the Quakers to appropriate to the same purpose a burial-ground belonging to them in Bunhill Fields has utterly failed. The ground was one which would have been of almost more value for the purpose than any I know in London. It is close to Whitecross Street, which some of you may know as a street quite swarming with costermongers; the houses there are tunnelled every few yards with archways leading to as crowded courts as I know anywhere. Many houses of the poor actually overlooked the ground. In Coleman Street, which bounds the ground on the north, is a factory from which crowds of workmen turn out daily at dinner-time, many, no doubt, to adjourn to the public-house. But one hot day last summer, when I was there, dozens of them were sitting on the dusty pavement, their backs leaning against the great, dead, heated wall, which hid from them the space occupied by the burial-ground. There is not a tombstone

in it, and it might have been planted and
thrown open easily.   Last summer I wrote
to the Quakers, hearing they were about to
sell the ground for building, laying before them
the reasons for devoting it to the public as
a garden.   After urging them to give it thus
to the poor themselves, I added a request
that if they did not see their way to do this,
they would at least pause to enable me and
my friends who were interested in such undertakings to see whether we could not raise
enough money to secure it for the poor, even
if they determined to exact for it full building-
land value.   I certainly could hardly believe
that Quakers could thus sell land once devoted
to their dead, and which had never brought
them in rent, but I thought it just possible
they might hesitate to give what belonged to
the Society all to the poor.   At any rate, I
was determined no want of effort on my part
should lose for the people so valuable and
unique a space lying in the heart of a crowded

neighbourhood. My letter was never even considered by the meeting. The company in treaty for the ground did not purchase it then, because they thought it irreverent to disturb the dead. Yet although I have again and again seen and written to leading Quakers about it, and addressed several letters to their organ, *The Friend*, they have deliberately just sold it for building. No builder could be found who liked to buy the ground and disturb the bodies, and the Quakers themselves employed workmen to accomplish the most ghastly un-earthing of the contents of the graves, up-rooting five thousand bodies, which, I should think, never was undertaken before. They are selling the land for dwellings for the poor, and are excusing themselves by harping on the need of dwellings; but the immediate neighbourhood is to be dealt with under the Artisans Dwellings Bill, by means of which a large number of healthy homes for the poor will be erected, while I fear there is no chance of any other garden being made in their midst. And, especially as only a portion of the Quakers' burial-ground is to be devoted to workmen's dwellings, the number of rooms provided in the district will not be sensibly affected. They have excused themselves, too, because they have not dug up George Fox, but only some of their lesser leaders and their nameless dead. Even if they formed a slightly different estimate of the relative advantages of a few more rooms and a garden, I own to an amazed sorrow that the Quakers rejected a scheme by which the land might have been rendered a blessing to the living, without doing violence to what seems to me to be a natural instinct of reverence, ineradicable in every human heart, for whatever has been associated with the loved, or the great and noble who are no longer with us. Nor could I have borne, if I had been they, to draw so marked a distinction between the unknown, who had surely been loved, and the known, who had been famous, as to uproot five thousand bodies and spare George Fox's grave. I am sorry English workmen were called in to "separate those who had lain side by side for two centuries," that "the bones of young and old were" by them "placed in coarse deal boxes and re-interred in a large hole at the other end of the ground." That "many of them, while awaiting this fresh burial, were piled in a rude heap in a corner," with carbolic acid poured over them. Is this the lesson our workmen are to learn? Are they, too, valueless because so nameless? These poor bodies now mouldering away were once animated by spirits of beloved men and women. That which was once the form which embodied any human soul, named or unnamed, would have seemed to me worth a little gentler care. Better have let it mingle quietly with the dust and feed the trees and the daisies, keeping the resting-place of the dead one also for the weary and the poor.

I deal with the matter thus at length because the Quakers still have a burial-ground
in Whitechapel and one in Bermondsey, which
would be available as gardens, and which
they have not yet sold ; and also because I
am not aware that they have decided how
they will deal with the small portion of the
Bunhill Fields ground which they cannot build
over, where they have re-buried their unearthed
dead.   Have any of you influence with them,
or can anything be done ?   The Whitechapel
ground, though not nearly so central and
important as Bunhill Fields, is well worth
preserving.   It is overlooked by the workhouse, in the chronic wards of which there
must be many who would rejoice to look out
over trees and flowers, and who will never
see them again unless this ground is planted
with them.   On the east side of the ground,
too, is a wall ; only to pull down that wall
and put a railing instead, would give light
and air to a whole street.   Yet though Mr.

Lefevre, on behalf of the Commons Preservation Society, has twice asked them to say
whether, and if so on what terms, they would
arrange for the ground to be put in order
and used as a garden for the people, they
give evasive answers, and I believe have it in
contemplation to sell it for building. The
rector of Whitechapel has written to them,
the guardians have memorialised them. They
make no responsive sign. I make these re-
marks in no spirit of hostility to the Quakers;
some of my oldest and best friends are Quakers,
and I have the deepest respect for them as
a body, and well know they have been leaders
in much that is good, thoughtful, and liberal
in times past, to the poor to a remarkable
degree, and I know the value of such gardens
is only beginning to attract notice; but I think
the facts as concerning the land should be
well known to the whole Society and to the
public, and I only hope that the Society will
consider them thoroughly at their yearly meet-

K

ing this month. Within the last few days
I have received letters from leading Quakers,
asking me to bring the question before their
yearly meeting; but I think I must really
leave it in their own hands; the responsibility
is wholly theirs. Their best ground is now
almost gone, the facts are well before them,
and Mr. Shaw-Lefevre's offer is not only well
known to the whole Society, but the corre-
spondence between him and their committee
has been published in *The Friend* newspaper.

There is another body which I hope will
swiftly become aware of their opportunities
for doing good with land which is under their
control—the London School Board. They
have in all fifty-seven acres of playground,
which they entirely close on the children's
one holiday, Saturday, and during the summer
evenings. It seems almost incredible, does
it not? But so it really is. Of course the
fact is that the Board has not considered how
to manage the supervision. But surely that

difficulty ought to be met either by the Board itself paying for it, if that is within its powers, or by some society, such as that which has summoned us here to-day, or by individual donors. Having the ground which, however small, is at least available for games for a certain number of children selected by the masters, it seems ridiculous not to use it. A deputation from this Society will wait on the School Board on May 30, to press the opening of the ground upon them—for that deputation influential support is much needed. If any of you can help, I hope you will communicate with Miss Lankester. I spoke of the very corrupting influence of the streets, though I did so with reference to the small companies of children who might be brought together for quiet pastimes in our churchyard-gardens of the future. The School Board playgrounds would afford scope for the more active games. Surely this should be afforded by anybody who realises how very beneficial

K 2

athletic exercise and active play would be to the children's health, and how happy it would make them. Why, I have seen two swings make children so happy, I have been ashamed to think how few we have in London. They don't take much space, and what delight they give!

A clergyman near here is about to fit up a yard as a gymnasium for the men belonging to a workmen's club, and doubtless others will do the same.

The uses to which even a small playground in London may be put would take long to describe. I have charge of two, where, besides opening them every Saturday and in the summer evenings, every May we have a real maypole—flowers from the country in thousands, flags flying, band playing, swings, and see-saws fully used, children marching, dancing, and skipping, and a kind and able body of ladies and gentlemen who know them amusing them, keeping order, and increasing by their presence the sense of festivity. The trustees of Lincoln's Inn Fields have, for the last two or three years, kindly granted to me leave to take in a company of the children of our tenants one afternoon each summer. It is a pleasant sight. The square is larger, I believe, than any in London, and the trees are most beautiful. They have also just given permission to the boys from the Refuge in Great Queen Street to exercise there two mornings a week from seven to nine o'clock. But this is a small amount of use to make of one of the largest, and most beautiful, and most central spaces of the metropolis, where there are few or no residents to be disturbed or interfered with at the hours when the ground would be most valuable; and it is to be earnestly hoped that the trustees will soon extend the privileges that they have hitherto kindly accorded to us to others. It appears to me to be simply a question of adequate supervision, and for this there are people who would be willing to pay.

It is well known that the Temple and
Lincoln's Inn Gardens are now opened regularly on summer evenings to children. Why
the managers limit the privilege to children I
cannot think   Surely older people need the
air, and surely they would help unconsciously
to keep order too.   The more of such places
that are open, the less will the grass in each
be worn—the better the people will learn to
behave.   I have sometimes heard it urged
against opening places to the poor that there
is a chance of their conveying infection to
children of a higher class.   Setting aside the
fact that out of doors is the last place people
are likely to take infection, and that I pre-
sume the richer children would be under supervision as to playing with strangers, I ask you
seriously to consider who ought to monopolise
the few spaces there are in this metropolis for
outdoor amusements.   Is it the children whose
parents take them to the sea, or the country,
or the Continent, when the summer sun makes

London unbearable? Is it the children who, if their little cheeks look pale, or their strength flags after an illness, are at once sent under careful supervision to Hastings or Malvern? Is it even the children whose sturdy and vigorous father has amassed a little money, and delights to take them by train on a Saturday afternoon to Richmond, Bushey, or Erith? Or is it not rather the tiny child of the hard-working widow, whose frail form seems almost to grow smaller year by year instead of larger? Is it not the pale child with great sunken eyes, just discharged from the hospital, the bed being wanted, convalescent, but to whom fresh air and a little quiet are still so needful? Is it not to the careful, motherly, little elder sister, patient nurse of eight or nine years old, hugging the heavy, round-cheeked baby, with two or three other children clinging to her dress, she who cannot get as far as the park? Is it not the sturdy urchin, son of a costermonger perhaps, whose hardy and

energetic spirit scorns the bounds of the narrow
court, and seeks wider fields with freer power
of movement, but who has no chance, even
when July comes, of climbing cliffs or jumping
ditches? Should not the few spaces be available for these latter to the very utmost of
your power? And again, do you really think
now, people who live in comfortable houses,
that you do or can escape infection by any
precautions if small-pox and fever rage in the
back courts of your city? You take all manner
of precautions, I know (except, perhaps, what
I should call the best of all), but you have
no idea how near you, how all round you, this
infection is, if it be indeed the subtle thing
doctors say. The shops you enter, the cabs
you travel in, the clothes you wear, the food
you eat, all bring you into communication
with those who are coming in contact with
patients whenever disease is rife. Depend on
it, your best chance of escape is to make the
places inhabited by the poor healthy, to let

them have open space where the fresh wind may blow over them and their clothes, places where they may be less crowded and gain health. You never will, or can, really separate yourselves from your neighbours; accept then the nobler aim of making them such that you shall desire not separation—but union.

Among the small open spaces which we must hope to see thrown open to the people in the time to come in a greater or less degree are the squares. Of course I know that the ground in the square gardens is the property of the freeholder, and that with the leases of the surrounding houses are granted certain privileges with regard to the gardens, which neither can nor ought to be arbitrarily withdrawn. But I hope the day is not far distant when it may dawn upon the dwellers in our West End squares that during August and September not one in fifty of their families is in town, and that it is a rather awful responsibility to lock up the only little bit of earth

which is unbuilt over, which is within reach
of the very old, the very feeble, or the very
young ; and that when they leave town they
will, in their corporate capacity, grant such
discretionary power to those who stay in town,
to admit the poor to sit under the trees, as
may seem consistent with their rights as lease-
holders, interpreted perhaps a little liberally,
as they contrast the utmost they *can* give in
the somewhat dingy, early dried-up, London
plane-tree, with the wealth of magnificent
foliage of wood, or park, or mountain, to
which they and their rejoicing family, baby
and all, grandmother and all, go before the
autumn sun dries up poor scorched London.

Also, oh, you rich people, to whom the
squares belong, some few of whom too own
private gardens actually in London, adjoining
Hyde Park or Regent's Park, or saved on
some great estate round the landowner's house,
I think you might have a flower-show or large
garden-party, once a year, for the poor of your

neighbourhood, while you are in town to meet them. I have seen such things done in squares with delightful results. A whole district gathered together, old friends and new, in happy fellowship under the trees, the band playing, and the place looking its gayest. I have seen tents filled with flowers reared in the houses of the poor, each in itself a poor plant, yet, gathered together, looking quite bright and flourishing; and friends whom circumstances had parted, former clergymen, former visitors, meeting the poor friend whom else it might have been difficult to see. Have such a party once a year if you can; one afternoon in the summer will never be missed by the dwellers in the square, while the memories of many a poor neighbour may be enriched by the thought of the bright gathering in the soft summer air. I never was present at the flower-shows at Westminster Abbey, nor do I know how far they grew out of previous intercourse with the poor; but I feel sure that is

the way to use any open space in London.
The more the festivals can be connected with
previous work the better; but those few who
own ground easily accessible to the people will
do well to put the ground once yearly at the
service of those who *do* know the poor for a
flower-show or garden-party. I know nothing
hat with less trouble gives more joy, or more
thoroughly brings corporate life into a parish.

There are, besides the grander squares, some,
I think, which are deserted by the rich, where
"life"—that is, plenty going on—would be more
acceptable than quiet; where the residents
would be actually glad to have the gates
thrown open, the beds set with bright flowers,
the seats available for all, as in Leicester
Square. I think even a band on a Saturday
afternoon might be thought a gain. It is a
pity these deserted wildernesses, with their
poverty-stricken privet-hedges, are not by some
common consent made to adapt themselves to
the needs of the neighbourhood.

I have thus far dwelt mainly on open spaces as affecting the health or social life of our people, but there is another way in which such spaces might be made most valuable to them. That is, if they could be made really beautiful. Londoners are surrounded with the most depressing ugliness; the richer ones try with more or less good taste to mitigate this by decoration indoors; but those who have little or no superfluous wealth, and far less refinement, to lead them to spend any part of it in this way, are, at home and abroad, from year's end to year's end, surrounded by ugliness. If we could alter this, it would go far to refine and civilise them. Now it would be difficult to do this in their own homes at once; besides, that is a sphere where each should do it for his own family; but wherever a common meeting-place is arranged, within doors or without, there it seems to me that rich people might find a really useful scope for spending money. The poor man's independence does not demand that he should plant trees and flowers for himself, or decorate with colour wall or door, still less does it require that he should provide such beautiful things for the public, rich or poor. My sister has founded a society, called, after the Man of Ross, the Kyrle Society, which has for its object to bring beauty into the haunts of the poor; it has met with much support, and I hope the day may come when hospitals, mission-rooms, school-rooms, workmen's clubs, and, in fact, all common meeting-places of the poor, may be enriched by beautiful things given by it. It is dealing also with open spaces, is not only planting and bringing plants to the poor, but it is trying in other ways to beautify these spaces, and I am not without hope that gradually either mural decorations, inscriptions in tiles, or possibly cloisters, might be given by those who cared to obtain for their fellow-citizens, not only space, but beauty. This is being done in some cases. I will read

you a short poem now being painted on zinc
by a lady, to put up on a wall of a tiny little
garden in a court in Whitechapel which is
under my care.

SONG OF THE CITY SPARROW.

When the summer-time is ended
  And the winter days are near ;
When the bloom hath all departed
  With the childhood of the year ;

When the martins and the swallows
  Flutter cowardly away,
Then the people can remember
  That the sparrows always stay.

That although we're plain and songless,
  And poor city birds are we,
Yet before the days of darkness
  We, the sparrows, never flee.

But we hover round the window,
  And we peck against the pane,
While we twitteringly tell them
  That the spring will come again.

And when drizzly dull November
  Falls so gloomily o'er all,
And the misty fog enshrouds them
  In a dim and dreary pall ;

When the streets all fade to dreamland,
  And the people follow fast,
And it seems as though the sunshine
  Was for evermore gone past ;

Then we glide among the house-tops,
  And we track the murky waste,
And we go about our business
  With a cheerful earnest haste.

Not as though our food were plenty,
  Or no dangers we might meet ;
But as though the work of living
  Was a healthy work and sweet.

When the gentle snow descendeth,
  Like a white and glistening shroud,
For the year whose life hath ended,
  Floated upwards like a cloud ;

Then although the open country
  Shineth very bright and fair,
And the town is overclouded,
  Yet we still continue there.

Even till the spring returneth,
  Bringing with it brighter birds,
Unto whom the city people
  Give their love and gentle words,

And we yet again, descended
  To become the least of all,
Take our name as "only sparrows,"
  And are slighted till we fall.

Still we're happy, happy, happy,
　　Never minding what we be ;
For we have a work and do it,
　　Therefore very blithe are we.

We enliven sombre winter,
　　And we're loved while it doth last,
And we're not the only creatures
　　Who must live upon the past.

With a chirrup, chirrup, chirrup,
　　We let all the slights go by,
And we do not feel they hurt us,
　　Or becloud the summer sky.

We are happy, happy, happy,
　　Never minding what we be,
For we know the good Creator
　　Even cares for such as we.

Is it not pleasant to think of the children
having those words to read—painted in pretty
colours, too—rather than looking at a blank
wall ? Sometimes I think we might even hope
to carry with us the hearts of people by setting
up for them deliberately very solemn and beautiful words indeed, coloured richly in lasting
tiles. I do not see why at any rate our
churches should not bear on their face some

L

message to the outside world. I was fancying the other day, as I looked at the great, blank, dirty, dead side wall of a London church, which was seen from a principal thoroughfare, and which bounded the graveyard, long disused, but full of graves, how beautiful it would be to put in coloured tiles, along the whole length of the wall, Kingsley's words:

> Do noble things, not dream them, all day long,
> And so make life, death, and that vast for-ever,
>   One grand, sweet song.

The words are simple, and would go home to the hearts of every passer-by ; the bright colours, the look of expensive care bestowed on them, the fact that they are on the wall of a church, would give them a look of serious purpose, too great, it seems to me, for any sense of jar as to their publicity to be felt for a moment. It seemed to me that as the hurrying crowd went its way along the thoroughfare, the words might recall to someone high purposes once entertained and long forgotten, either in the struggle of life or the more deadening influence of success or ease—startle him to memories, at least, of a greater, nobler life than he was leading ; to the weary and dejected it seemed to me they might point to the continuance in that great hereafter of all we seem to lose here, and all the while the words would be felt to be keeping watch over the dead, whose sudden silence is so hard to bear, but the harmony of whose grand, sweet song in that vast for-ever we catch now and again when we *are* doing noble things, and so tuning our hearts into more perfect sympathy with the music of God's universe.

I have spoken mainly of making open spaces, because I think the usefulness of the parks and the embankment is much more generally known. I am rather afraid of their being supposed to supersede the need of small open spaces quite near the homes of the poor, than of their value being underrated. The old and the very young cannot get to them often,

nor from all parts of London. But I ought
hardly to pass them over in absolute silence ;
they certainly do meet a quite distinct want
on the part of the stronger portion of the
community, who can get some sense of power
of expansion, can see the fair summer sun
going down behind the towers. of Westminster
Abbey, a space of sky being visible, so rarely
seen from the streets or courts. Let us be very
thankful for them.

Also when I undertake to speak to you
about open spaces, though I cannot to-day
dwell on them at length, I dare not omit all
reference to those which are perhaps most
precious of any, and which are by no means
secured to us as yet as the parks are—our
commons — the only portion of the land of
England which remains in a living sense of the
birthright of the people of England, and which,
bit by bit, gradually and insidiously is filched
away, under this and that pretext, by one big
landowner after another, quietly surrounded by

his effectual railing, and added to his park or field. Often is this done under shadow of law, often without any legal right, but just because no one is careful enough, or rich enough, or brave enough to oppose. My friends, there is a society which has done much good work, much unpopular work, which this session even saved you from encroachments on Mitcham and Barnes Commons ; it is little known, it wants money support, and it deserves your full support of every kind—the Commons Preservation Society. Note down its address, 1, Great College Street, Westminster, give it what support you can, but above all if ever you see a common threatened, or a piece of one inclosed, write and ask the Society whether it is legally done—what chance of redress there is. The Society has set itself to fortify local effort by advice, by parliamentary support, sometimes by money; it watches over the interests of Englishmen in the small amount of uninclosed land yet remaining to them.

While house is being added to house and field to
field, while one small farm after another is
being swallowed up in the big estate, there are
yet left for the common inheritance of Englishmen who have small chance of ever owning
even a little garden of their very own, some
few moorland spaces, set with gorse and
heather, fringed by solemn rank of guardian
fir-trees, where in the sandy banks their children
yet may hollow caves, where the heath-bell
waves in the faint evening breeze, and from
which—oh, wondrous joy to us Londoners—still
the far blue distance may be seen, witness
to us for ever, as it lies there still, and calm,
and bright, that the near things which over-
shadow us, which seem so tremendous, like tall
London houses, built by man, and covering so
large a portion of our horizon and sky, hemming
us in with terrible oppressive sense of dreari-
ness, may fade back and back from us in
distance, till they become even lovely in God's
fair sunlight, little jagged peaks only against

His calm sky, and all softened into sweetest colour by the light He sheds over them.

Keep those fair, far, still places for your children, and your children's children, if you can : the more cities increase, the more precious they will be ; for the more man's soul will long for the beauty, for the quiet, which the city does not, cannot give.

VII.

EFFECTUAL CHARITY.*

TENDER pity for the poor has been a growing
characteristic of this age ; a better sign of it
still is the increased sense of duty to them, not
only as *poor* men, but as *men*. There needs,
however, it appears to me, something still
before our charity shall be effectual for good.
The feeling is there, the conscience is there,
but there is wanting the wise thought and
the resolute, because educated, will.

Our charity, if by the word we mean our
loving-kindness, has been good in itself, but if
we mean by the word, alms-giving, can we

* Paper read at a meeting of the Charity Organisation Society,
at Highgate, June 18th, 1877.

flatter ourselves that it has been productive of a satisfactory state of things? We have taught our poor to live in uncertainty as to their resources, which is producing among them a reckless want of forethought, which is quite appalling. The most ordinary occurrences of their lives—the regular winter frost which stops the work of some men year by year; the changes in the labour market, caused by the London season; the expenses attending illness; the gradual approach of old age—are not dwelt on now usually among the poor as reasons for trying to provide a fund to meet them. Thus there are hundreds of our people living on the extremest brink of pauperism or starvation, learning more and more to be dependent on the chance coal-ticket, or half-crown, or blanket; and if it does not happen to be given at the moment when it is wanted, how forlorn is the position of the improvident man? But look also on the even more important question of their spirit, and of their

relation to those above them in class.   Can
there be energy, independence, vigour, healthy
activity among them?   Can there be between
them and the donors any of that happy manly
interchange of thought, by which the pos-
sessors of education, refinement, leisure, might
help, or be helped by, the active, self-reliant
working-man, with his large capacity for fresh
vigorous joy, and his store of power accumulated during a long period of endurance and
patient effort?   If different classes, like different
people, have separate characters which are
meant to act and react one on the other, are
we not, by allowing the help to be one of a
dole of money, destroying the possibility of
the better help that might have been?

And is our money doing any good?   Did
you ever see the district—the family—the individual that was richer for this repeated alms-
giving?   Has it ever been powerful, even for
outside good, to be recipients?   Is the bed
better covered in the long run for the lent

blankets, or the children better fed for the free distribution of soup? Or is it consistent with our ideal that there should be this body of people dependent for the most ordinary necessities of life on the gifts of another class? Rely upon it, if we foster this state of things it will continue to increase.

Here we are, however, in the midst of this alms-giving, aimless, thoughtless, ineffectual to achieve any object its donors had in view. It is a gigantic system, or rather no system, which has grown up around us. What is our duty with regard to it? Specially what is the duty of those of us who are, in any sense of the word, trustees of charitable funds?

There is a society which you all know well enough by name — the Charity Organisation Society—which has set itself to help distributors of alms in two important ways. First, it has offered to examine, free of all charge, carefully, for anyone who wants to learn about them, the circumstances and character of ap-

plicants for relief. Donors cannot decide what
help it is wise to give until they know all
about an applicant ; the Society can learn
such facts in a far more complete way than
donors possibly can. Clearly then, to my
mind, donors or distributors of gifts ought to
accept this proffered help.

But the Society offers a second advantage ;
it will give an opinion on the case of an
applicant. When the facts respecting his condition and character are ascertained, the problem is simply this. How can he be so helped
that the help may soon be needed no longer ;
how placed speedily out of the reach of want,
in an honourable useful place where he can help
himself ? Or if his need be necessarily chronic,
how can he be provided for adequately and
regularly—so regularly that he shall be tempted
neither to begging nor extravagance ? It is
very difficult to set a man up again in the
world ; and the main hope of doing it is to
pause deliberately over his case, to bring to

bear upon it all the collected information, all the practised experience, and intelligent thought of men and women accustomed to think out such problems, and to watch the results of many attempts to solve them. The ordinary district visitor has no qualifications for forming an opinion on the best way of meeting the difficulties of the case, nor usually has the busy clergyman much more. The visitor has very rarely even a glimmering notion that there is such a way of dealing with the poverty she pities, she hardly dreams that it is possible to attack it at its roots, and so she gives the ticket or the shilling. The clergyman usually feels that this is an unsatisfactory way of treating the matter; but he knows probably no more than the visitor, in what part of the country there may be an opening for work for the man whose trade is slack in London; nor what training would enable the invalid girl who can only use her hands, and lies bed-ridden and helpless, to contribute something to the common income ; nor what institution would receive, and how the guardians might pay for, the cripple who is made an excuse for begging for the whole family, and how he might learn a trade, and in the future honourably support himself.   It is only a body accustomed to deal with many such cases, to devote attention to practical questions mainly, that acquires the knowledge of what measures can be taken under different circumstances, and knows the latest news as to the labour market, and the opportunities open to the needy.

I am far from saying that the Charity Organisation Society has, as yet, in each of the thirty-eight divisions of London, a committee capable of giving a valuable opinion on a case ; nor even that in every district the committee has realised that to give such an opinion is its real end and aim.   But I do say that this is the intention of the Society, and that on the committee, if anywhere, you will in each neighbourhood find the men and women most alive to the importance of fulfilling this duty; for more and more of the district committees are finding members who set before themselves the necessity of learning to execute it.

I know little of your own Charity Organisation Committee, but I would ask you to remember that it is not a separate society coming from afar and settling down among you. It is what you workers among the poor make it; it is you who ought to form it. And that which I said above you separately were not able to do, collectively you, and none but you, can do—decide what help it is wise to give to every poor man or woman who comes before you at a crisis in life. A representative from every local charity, a few men conversant with the work of every great metropolitan charity, two or three active guardians, the clergy and ministers of all denominations, or some leading member of their staff or congregations, these should form your district committee. After careful investigation by a skilled paid officer, the case of an applicant for charity, when it comes before such a committee as that, has a fair chance of really effectual treatment. Either someone present will know of work that needs to be done ; or, if the applicant's wants can only be met by distinct gift, then, all the givers or their representatives being present, the gift can after due deliberation be made without chance of overlapping, with certainty that it is sufficient and its object well thought out.

District visitors will find it valuable to study with the district committee many questions respecting relief. The work of visitors is one in which I have long taken the deepest interest ; their gentle influence in their informal visits is just what is wanted to bridge over the great chasm which lies open between classes. Rich and poor should know one another simply and naturally as friends, and the more visitors can enter into such real friendship the better. When, however, they attempt to deal with cases of relief, I feel that they possess few of the qualifications requisite for doing it wisely, and I would most seriously urge them, either to leave this branch of help entirely to others, or with deliberate purpose to set themselves to learn all that it is essential to them to know before they can do it well. For there is more at stake, a great deal more, than the wasting of their own or their friends' money: that would matter comparatively little if the effect of mistake in its use were not positively disastrous to the poor. But it is disastrous. We go into the house of a young working-man; we meet with ready gift the first need as it arises; we do not pause to remember how the effort to meet that need was a duty for the young husband and father. We discourage the quiet confidence, the careful forethought which would have made a man of him; we diminish his sense of responsibility; the way he spends his earnings begins to appear to him a matter of smaller moment—

M

he dissipates them in the public-house ; he
gets into the habit of doing so ; we, or succeeding visitors, feel the hopelessness of help
increase ; not only does the drag upon our
purse become heavier and heavier, but it
becomes clearer to us that the money we
give does not adequately feed the wife and
children, while it does lead the husband to
hope that if he yields to the strongly increased
temptation to drink, some lady will help,
some charity interpose, the children won't
quite starve. We have weakened the natural
ties, broken the appointed order, and the neat,
tidy little home has sunk into the drunkard's
desolate room.

Or we take up the case of a widow, and
instead of once for all considering how much
she can do for her own and her children's
support, and deliberately uniting our forces to
relieve her once for all of that part of the
cost which she cannot meet, we let her come
up to our house whenever she cannot fulfil

her engagements, and we give her, when her story or tears move us, a few shillings. We ease our own feelings by doing this, but what besides have we done. We have not fortified her for the battle of life ; we have not cultivated in her the habit of deliberate arrangement as to the best expenditure of her scanty means. We have done something to teach her how easy it is, if she gets into debt and the brokers are put in, to go round to one house after another and get a few shillings from each, and having met the difficulty for the moment to begin involving herself in another. Look at her a few years later. The sincere grief of the widowed mother has been degraded into a means of begging ; the ready tears come, or appear to come, at call ; the sacred grief is for everyone to see in hopes someone may alleviate it with half-a-crown. The sense of a right to be helped has grown, the sense of her own duty has diminished. Work has not paid so well that it has been steadily persevered in. The easily begged money has been easily spent; the powers of endurance, the habits of industry are gone; grief is her stock-in-trade; its frequent use has diminished the power of feeling strongly and sincerely. Perhaps she has discovered that professions of piety are rewarded with half-crowns, and expressions, once sincere, have become cant phrases. We are shocked at her; we say we were glad enough to help her when she was working, and was feeling simply and strongly, but now it is different. My friends, who made it different? God gave her the sacred sorrow and the difficulties of her life to soften and to train her. It might have been well that we should like true friends have stood by her, and so far diminished her difficulty as to make it just within her power to meet it; it might have been well for us to support one child, to pay school-fees, or to help in some other way by some one distinct payment, so regular as to become very natural to her, but in some way we ought to have left her responsibilities to have been met by her own energies. Then we should have been able to take and keep the position of friends ; she would not have learned to watch our faces to see what expression on her part extorted pity or shillings best, but would have come to us when the memories of the past were too heavy to bear alone, and the words of hope in God's mercy and wisdom would have been spoken from the heart to the heart.

Let visitors be friends, and nothing else, leaving money help to others ; or else study seriously all wise effectual ways of help, that they may not be driven to miserable doles of half-crowns and bread-tickets, which are surely destructive of vigorous life in the poor, and of natural healthy relation between friends. I could, you could yourselves, multiply instances of this a hundredfold. It will be more profitable to study how in the future they may be avoided.

A marked advantage of district committees is that, while doing nothing to weaken local action, they present a larger area to the sympathy of their members. When parishes were first constituted, each parish must in general have had its own rich and poor. But this has ceased to be so in many cases, owing to the large population dwelling in a small area. The tendency of late has been to subdivide ecclesiastical districts. The rich are not anxious to have the poor living in very close proximity to them, and every class is more and more driven into quarters appropriated exclusively to itself. The consequence of this is—and increasingly—that if a rich man says, "I will help in my own parish," there are vast numbers of poor living perhaps near to him, probably within what in the country would be considered easy walking distance, and certainly in the same town, whose lives he does not touch. I cannot tell you how terrible to me appear these

vast spaces of ground covered with houses
inhabited by persons at one dead level of
poverty ; sometimes the tracts appropriated
to the houses of the wealthy seem to me in
another way more terrible. All good gifts,
for which we are bound to lift our hearts in
praise to God, seem to retain their sanctity
only when they are shared ; and it seems to
me often as if the luxury, the ease, the
splendour, yes, even the fair spaces of lawn
and terrace were almost ghastly when they
are enjoyed by those who never consider the
poor, in whom no spirit of self-sacrifice leads
to resolute appropriation of some large share
of the good things to those who are out of
the way. There are few who do not recognise the duty of giving or sharing in some
measure ; but the subdivision of districts, leaving
one poor and another rich, the ever-extending
size of London making the poor farther and
farther off from the rich, has a tendency to
shut out many poor from this sympathy.

The Charity Organisation Society has done
something to mitigate this evil, to make you
feel that you are parts of a larger whole than
your ecclesiastical parish.   The poor-law has
compulsorily made you feel it.   When it became
clear that it was intolerably unjust to throw
the burden of the largest number of paupers
on the poorest ratepayers, poor-law areas
were enlarged so as to unite rich and poor
neighbourhoods ; also, certain expenditure was
charged to a metropolitan rate.   That poor-
law arrangement, however, never touched your
hearts.   It is doubtful whether the dwellers
in Fitzroy Park feel more united with those
in Somer's Town because they are both in
St. Pancras parish, nor much added tender-
ness for the sick man in Poplar, because if he
has small-pox he is carried to a hospital supported by a metropolitan rate.   The alteration
has done good because it has equalised burdens,
and enforced the fulfilment of a duty.   But
the Charity Organisation Society does more—

it asks you to accept this duty as a privilege, and voluntarily and gladly to help, remembering the less favoured districts which are near you, or which, though farther off, still belong to the same city. It has taken the poor-law boundary to mark its area; it has asked all charitable people within that area to meet and consult about their charities; it has arranged that the working expenses of office and agent shall be shared by a large district, it has formed a meeting-place, where workers for the poor shall be able to learn each what the other is doing, even at the farther extremes of a long parish like this. You will certainly enlarge your sympathies if thus you meet; for when, there come before you the stories of living men and women wanting help in districts where funds are not abundant, when you learn to know the clergy and others labouring in poorer places, you will begin to interpret the word "neighbour" in a large and liberal sense.

Do you realise how limited is our notion of it now, and what it has brought us to? Have you any picture before you of the parts of London where for acres and acres the ground is covered with the dwellings of the poor alone, where no landlord can afford many feet of space unbuilt over at the back of his house; where the clergyman toils on almost singlehanded, for unrefreshed year after unrefreshed year; where curates will hardly go and work; where no gay life enlivens the monotony of toil, which is interrupted only by the wild unholy carousal of a Bank holiday; where the clergyman's wife can hardly sleep because of the wild mirth of the surrounding streets? We talk of the claims of parish and neighbourhood, and they should be seriously remembered; but are they not sometimes urged rather from a lazy desire not to take the trouble to go farther, or from the easy agreeable wish to oblige the neighbouring minister, who calls to ask a new resident for help in the Sunday school or district? If, indeed, the decision is a deliberate choice of a near duty distinctly seen, rather than of a far off one less realised, one 'may respect it. But we must remember there are other claims than those arising out of proximity, and that it may be our duty to realise what is not brought under our eyes. We live upon the labours of the poor in districts far from our homes. Our fathers and brothers may have chambers, factories, offices right down among them. We are content to draw our wealth from these. Does this imply no duty? Is the whole duty fulfilled when the head of a firm draws a cheque for donations to the local charity, and are the gentle ministrations of the ladies of the family to be confined to the few pampered poor near their house? It is our withdrawal from the less pleasant neighbourhood to build for ourselves substantial villas with pleasant gardens, which has left these tracts what they are. Even when there

is nothing sensationally terrible in the wicked-
ness or destitution of a place, when it is covered
with little houses of laundresses or small shop-
keepers, are we who have advantages of education or refinement not needed there? Have
we no bright flowers to take to the people,
no books to lend, no sweet sympathy and
young brightness to carry among them?
Ought we not to be accumulating those
memories which will give us a place near
them as real friends if the time of loss and
trial comes?

I would urge you all who are inhabitants
of a large parish, markedly divided into poor
and rich districts, as citizens of a city fear-
fully so divided, to weigh well your duties;
and, never forgetting the near ones to home
and neighbourhood, to remember also that
when Europe is sacrificed to England, England to your own town, your own town to
your parish, your parish to your family, the
step is easy to sacrifice your family to your-

self. Whereas if you try to accept the duty as our Lord showed it, and to carry with you joyfully in such acceptance those who are nearest and dearest to you, you will find that a large and true imagination will show you the place which every duty should hold in your lives; you will not find any human being so away but that your sympathy will reach, and your desire to help will tell in due degree if the need of help comes. Your life, be it shadowed ever so much by individual loss or pain, will be full and blessed; for all God's children will be dear to you, and His earth sacred; you will have no real conflict of duties, nor long doubt about their relative importance; no pain shall overwhelm, nor doubt confound you; for the blessing of guidance shall be yours, and you will assuredly learn what those words mean, "When thou passest through the waters I will be with thee, and through the rivers they shall not overflow thee." "Though the Lord give thee the bread of adversity, and the water of affliction, yet shall not thy teachers be re- moved into a corner any more; but thine eyes shall see thy teachers, and thine ears shall hear a word saying, This is the way, walk ye in it, when ye turn to the right hand or when ye turn to the left."

VIII.

THE FUTURE OF OUR COMMONS.

THE question of the appropriation of the common land of England is one which is of great importance now, and which will be of increasing importance as time goes on. The matter is not simply one of providing a public park or common in the near neighbourhood of cities which are now large and rapidly increasing, nor of securing a cricket or recreation ground and an acre or two of cottage gardens to a few villagers. The question before the country—and it is well we should realise its magnitude before ⬛⬛⬛⬛⬛ sions are made—is whether ⬛⬛⬛⬛ all private rights, the⬛⬛⬛

England which can be preserved for the common good ; and, secondly, in what way such
land can best be used. Is it best to parcel
it out amongst various owners, and increase
the building or corn-growing area? Is it best
to let the largest possible amount of it in
allotments to the poor? Is it well to devote
any portion of it, in rural as well as suburban
districts, to the public, to be by them enjoyed
in common, in the form of beautiful, wild, open
space?

It must be observed that the nation as a
nation is not held to possess the open, unculti-
vated, unappropriated land of England. True,
generation after generation has passed over
much of it freely, but it seems that the people
are not thereby held to have acquired a right
to do so. Perhaps this is because such right
has no money value, for rights of way, rights
of light, rights of possession of soil, even rights
on these very open spaces of pasturing cattle,
cutting furze and of playing games are recog-

nised by law when they have been long enjoyed. Had the right to wander freely, and to enjoy the beauty of earth and sky, been felt to be a more distinct possession, it may be that these rights also would have been legally recognised; but it has not hitherto been so. It is, therefore, lords of manors and commoners who have mainly the control of such waste places. When, however, they come to Parliament to ask to have their respective rights settled, and to get leave to inclose, Parliament has, under the Inclosure Acts, distinctly a voice in deciding the appropriation of the land. What ought its decision to be, having in view the future life of the nation as well as the present one?

That æsthetic considerations govern individuals in the disposition of their own estates is clear. When a gentleman possesses an estate he apportions it to various uses. He asks himself how much of it he will devote to arable land and kitchen garden; some small

N

part he may set aside for his children, that they may dig in it and plant it in their spare time ; and a part of it he will devote probably to a flower-garden or a park ; for he knows that the family has need of enjoyment and of rest, and that beauty sustains in them some higher life than the mere material one. Are we as a nation to have any flower-garden at all ? Can we afford it ? Do we care to set aside ground for it, or will we have beet-root and cabbages only ? In other words, is all the land, so far as the people are concerned, from sea to sea, to be used for corn-growing, or building over only ? Are those who own estates to have their gardens, and the people to have none ? or, if any, how many and how pretty may they be ? Is there only land enough for exercise near the big city, or can we have any for beauty far away from it ?

Surely we want some beauty in our lives ; they cannot be all labour, they cannot be all feeding. When the work is done, when the

eating is finished, the soul and spirit of men
ask for rest; they want air, they want the
sense of peace, they want the sense of space,
they want the influence of beauty. Men seek
it on the rocky sea-shore, on the peaks of
the mountains, by the streams in the valleys,
or on the heather-covered moorlands. Over-
excited in the cities, over-strained by toil,
they need, if it were but once in their lives,
that wonderful sense of pause and peace which,
the near presence of the great creations of
God gives. The silence brings them mar-
vellous messages, the clouds seem their com-
panions, the lights which pass over the
heather-covered hills fill them with an im-
measurable joy. Old cares seem so far away
as hardly to be real; and in the great peace
which surrounds them the whole spirit is
brought into harmony with grander music,
tuned to nobler imaginings, and nerved for
mightier struggles. "Man does not live by
bread alone." And the words God speaks to

us on the moorlands proceed, indeed, from His mouth with audible power, and memories of them haunt us with ennobling and consoling thought in the bustle, the struggle, and the pain to which we must return. This as individuals we know. There are signs that, as a Nation, we are beginning to see it.

A very remarkable change with regard to the relative value of different uses of land has taken place in England during the last thirty years, as the course taken by the Legislature sufficiently proves. Mr. Cross, in introducing the Commons Act of last year, laid stress upon this change. He pointed out that the Inclosure Act of 1845 was framed when the notion of statesmen was that England must depend, at any rate in case of war, wholly on herself for the wheat which her people needed. The Corn Laws were not then repealed; the country was not nearly so thickly populated; space was far more abundant; and the production of wheat seemed the best possible use to which land could be devoted. It was far different now. Corn reached our shores untaxed ; our population had so vastly increased that it necessarily depended largely on imported wheat; we had learned much more about the importance to health of fresh air and exercise, and we felt increasingly the value of space as well as food for our people. The needs of the nation in 1845 demanded inclosure for purposes of cultivation, and the Act of that year was accordingly specially drawn to facilitate it. But now the case was different, and Mr. Cross stated that his Bill was specially intended to promote regulation to meet the growing need of open space.

Further proof of the change in public opinion is afforded by the course taken by Parliament with regard to the New Forest. In 1851 no public objection was raised to an Act which was passed, empowering the Crown to plant formal and monotonous plantations of fir-trees, valuable as timber, in such a manner as eventually to cover the whole expanse of forest; while in 1876 this Act was repealed in favour of one which provided that the ancient trees and wild undergrowth should be left henceforward undisturbed; thus showing that the nation is now willing to sacrifice the profits accruing from fast-growing timber in order to preserve forest glades and heathery slopes, valuable only for their beauty.

The advantages to the Nation of possessing uninclosed land in perpetuity in certain instances, as opposed to the advantage of cultivating every available acre, have thus been distinctly recognised. But the proportion and situation of such uninclosed land remains to be determined, and will be decided by Parliament in the course of the next year or two.

Mr. Cross's Act prescribes that the application for regulation or inclosure shall be made to the Inclosure Commissioners (who were appointed under the Act of 1845), the

Commissioners are to hold a local inquiry, and then prepare a scheme which is to be submitted to a committee of the House. The scheme, when approved by the committee, comes before the House for confirmation. It may prove unfortunate that agents originally selected to administer an Act having for its main object *inclosure*—*i.e.* the dividing of the land among separate owners—should have been chosen to carry out one specially intended, as Mr. Cross explained, to facilitate *regulation* —*i.e.* the preserving of the land open for the use of all.

So great has been the tendency to inclose that, out of 414,000 acres available for allotments, recreative-grounds, &c., under the Act of 1845, only 4,000 had actually been thus allotted; whilst in 1869, out of 6,916 acres proposed to be inclosed, such were the views of the Commissioners, that they considered nine acres to be adequate reservation for public purposes—viz. three for recreation, and

six for field-gardens. And the four schemes
hitherto submitted to Parliament under the
new Act contained a provision for only seven-
teen acres to be reserved for recreation and
sixty-five for field-gardens out of 6,000 to be inclosed. The lords of the manors subsequently
offered two more in each case, if opposition
in committee were withdrawn. The offer was
accepted by the committee, but the attempt
to pass the Bill at the fag end of the session
was most fortunately frustrated.

There is yet time, therefore, for consideration whether regulation would not meet
the requirements of some of these cases
rather than inclosure; and in some of them,
or at least those parts of them which are
commons or waste lands of manors strictly
speaking, as distinguished from commonable
lands, it would seem that if ever regulating
schemes are to be adopted in rural districts,
these are cases most suitable for them.

One of the commons recommended for inclosure—Riccall Dam—is pasture land, and will never be available for growing corn, as it is subject to floods. It is close to the village, and is constantly used for cricket. The chief objection to its present condition is that the existing rights of turning out cattle upon it are improperly used, an evil which it is admitted could be remedied by regulation. If such an open space is to be inclosed, it is difficult to conceive what rural common, in the opinion of the Inclosure Commissioners, would be a fit subject for regulation.

The conviction is forced upon us that, unless the Inclosure Commissioners insist upon regulation wherever it is practicable, there will be little prospect of this part of the recent Act having a fair trial. Those who are pecuniarily interested in the commons—the lords of the manors and the commoners—will, as a rule, prefer inclosure to regulation, and the bias of the Commis-

sioners will probably be in the same direction ;
and if the option rests only with them there
is little doubt which course will be preferred.

It behoves, then, the Commissioners to
carry out the intentions of Mr. Cross, and
to refuse inclosure in any case where regulation may be applicable, and not to act
only upon the instance and preferment of
those interested. The failure so far of the
regulating clauses of the Act of 1876 bears
out the views of those who opposed the Act,
and who, while conceding the good intents of
the promoters, pointed out that the regulating
clauses were so hampered by the necessity of
consents that they practically presented no
alternative to inclosure, and who predicted that
few, if any, schemes would ever come before
Parliament under this part of the Act.

It has been shown that in all probability
thirty-seven schemes for inclosure come before
Parliament next session. Many thousands of
acres now open will be subjected to in-

closure under these schemes, and they will form the precedent for dealing with others in the future. They will come before Parliament; but the evidence in each case is heard only by a small committee; and there are but few outside that committee who will notice or care anything about each scheme as it successively comes forward. And yet, if the schemes are all carried out, England will have next year from this cause alone thirty-seven fewer open spaces than she has hitherto possessed. A great deal of this land might be saved if public attention were aroused, and aroused in time. On the next two or three years the fate of our commons will mainly depend. For seven years past, pending legislation, it has been possible to resist all schemes for inclosure; but since the passing of the Act of 1876 postponement of action is no longer possible, and each scheme must be dealt with immediately, and on its own merits.

There is danger lest, as the schemes may

relate each to a small area, and may not come before the public simultaneously, the gravity of the issue may not be generally perceived. It is no less a one than what proportion of the soil of England—of its commons, charts, and forests, its scars, fells, and moorlands—shall be retained to be used in common by her people as open unappropriated space both now and in the time to come.

Such, however, has been the growth of public opinion, that we may assume that Parliament would not sanction the inclosure of a common in the near neighbourhood of any large and populous town. But there seems some danger lest our legislators and the public should not duly consider how rapid is the growth of many towns, and that some which are not large and closely packed now may in a few years become so, and may need commons in their vicinity; nor how in many places suburb stretches beyond suburb as year succeeds year, and thus the town approaches the commons which once were rural. Increased facilities of swift and inexpensive travelling, and the opening of new lines of railway, make many a common once out of reach of the dwellers in town practically easy of access.

And there is a reason why even the still more distant rural commons should if possible be saved from inclosure. Every year, in many country neighbourhoods, population is increasing, and houses for letting are being built; more and more the field-paths by the river-side are being closed, and the walks through the cornfields or bright upland meadows are being shut. The hedge through the many gaps of which it was easy once to step into the roadside-wood and to gather primroses in thousands is now stoutly repaired, and new boards are put up warning trespassers that they "will be prosecuted." In self-defence the landowners erect barriers and warn off the public wherever that public becomes numerous.

The field shut up for hay in the remote country has so small a chance of being trampled on, that the farmer, hospitably or carelessly, leaves the gate unlocked; but as the neat little rows of lodging-houses come to be built near it, or as substantial villas multiply in the neighbourhood, and the buttercups tempt the more numerous little children to run in among the tall grass near the path, or the great boughs of may induce the big boys to make long trampled tracks beside the hedge, the farmer is obliged to lock his gate, put up his notices, or, if "right of way" exist, erect a fence which should leave the narrowest admissible pathway for the public. So it is, so it will be, year by year increasingly, with all private property. It is not only the artisan who, on his day's holiday, will depend more and more on the common or public park; the professional man, the shopkeeper who is able to take a house or lodgings for a few weeks in August or September for his family, will

also depend more and more each year on
finding some neighbourhood where there is a
heath, or forest, or moor which is public. He
does not take his wife and children away only
to breathe fresher air, nor is the small lodging-
house garden all they want to spend the day
in. To walk merely along the roads, if these
roads pass between parks or fields barricaded
from entrance, frets the human love of freedom
which makes us want to wander farther, to
escape the dusty prescribed track, to break
away over the hills, or pause in the meadow
by the pool or the river, or gather the
flowers in the wood. The more these are and
must be closed, the more intensely precious
does the common or forest, safe for ever from
inclosure, become. It is not only the suburban
common, it is the rural also which is of value
to us as a people.

Nor does the allotment scheme, admirable
as it is in giving the landless classes a share
in our common soil, in the least degree meet

the need for beauty. Under all the schemes for inclosing rural commons, it is probable that henceforward provision will be made for field-gardens. This is excellent. But do not let it be supposed that such allotments compensate for the entire loss of all open unappropriated land.

It is, moreover, possible that allotments might, as time goes on, be provided from quite other sources than our commons. The very considerable area held in trust for charitable purposes may well furnish ground for the purpose. Moreover, future changes which should facilitate the transfer of land, and should enable men to buy or rent it in small quantities, would meet the demand for allotments. Such changes might easily be effected when Englishmen come to the conclusion that small gardens are desirable for the people. If the allotments are not made now we may still hope for them in the future; but if we lose our open spaces now, shall we ever recover them? Think of the cost of purchasing them back! Think of the compulsory powers to compel sale of contiguous plots! Think of the impossibility of breaking them ever again into uneven surface of woodland, dingle, or old quarry, or getting the forest trees on them again; and pause before you barter them for a few cultivated gardens, rented at high rates to a small group of men—valuable as field-gardens in themselves maybe.

Note, too, by-the-way, what is done in giving them. For allotments, working-men will pay four or five times the agricultural value and have done so, under the old Inclosure Acts. That proves them to be appreciated. Under the recent Act the amount of payment is limited. But is it not strange to take away free enjoyment from many, and to offer in exchange, at any money payment, a privilege to the few?

We have mentioned the schemes of inclosure now coming before the Legislature, but

o

besides these there is another extensive process of inclosure going on for which the Legislature is not responsible. It is that which is silently pursued by lords of manors, without any distinct legal settlement of rights. They *may* be taking only their due; they may be taking more. In some cases they are offering to the commoners, or to the poor, where lands are left for their benefit, gifts of money or land or coals, in lieu of their old rights of cutting fuel or turning out a cow. Perhaps the coals are quite equivalent to the value of the fuel to the individual cottager; but they depend often on the will of squire or lord, are administered by churchwardens to the needy, and become a form of dole instead of a birthright. Again, all land in England is increasing in value. Why should the ignorant agricultural labourer be induced, by the gift of a few poles of land, to part with the valuable inheritance of his descendants? Why should the lord absorb to himself alone the "unearned increment of the land?" It ought not to be left to any private person to make such terms with his tenants, still less ought he to be allowed to decide, by high-handed erection of fence, how much is his and how much is theirs. Yet there are numbers of such inclosures silently going on throughout England in districts where there is no one powerful enough, rich enough, or with knowledge enough to carry the matter into a court of law, or watch effectually that justice be done. Such suits are very costly; the law in such cases is often complicated; a large amount is needed to secure the plaintiff against loss should he not have costs awarded him; and landowners, knowing that these difficulties prevent their being opposed when they inclose the tempting ground adjoining their park, and give a little bit of it to all neighbours likely to be troublesome, too often exercise a power which there is no one at hand to prevent.

Even the metropolitan commons, which might

have been thought to be already secured by the Metropolitan Commons Act of 1866, are not absolutely safe. No one now would apply for leave to inclose one of these *into to*, but there is hardly a company advocating a scheme for a reservoir or sewage farm, sidings for a railway or what not, that does not cast longing eyes on the cheap common land, one little bit of which it is supposed will hardly be missed. Accordingly, application is made to Parliament for compulsory power to take a small portion. So our metropolitan commons even may be nibbled away, and polluted and spoilt by the proximity of objectionable buildings or works. No less than five such schemes came before the public in 1877 affecting Barnes, Mitcham, and Hampstead.

The reader will perceive from what has been said that three distinct dangers threaten our common land :—

1st. That due use should not be made of the powers given by the Act of last year, to promote regulation rather than inclosure, and that in the separate schemes about to be presented to Parliament no weight whatever should be given to the growing importance of wild open spaces free to all.

2nd. That illegal inclosure should take place unnoticed, or be unopposed, for want of legal knowledge or money to organise resistance.

3rd. That the commons already protected by the Metropolitan Commons Act should be injured by the action of bodies applying for compulsory powers of purchase for small portions of them.

It remains only to consider what can be done to meet these three dangers.

First. Let the public take care that they thoroughly understand the bearings of every scheme submitted to Parliament. Let due notice be taken that the proportion of land allotted to the public be adequate, and that the situation of it be well selected. Much depends also on its character. To revert to the parallel of the disposition of land made by the owner of an estate, who certainly would not place his kitchen - garden in the loveliest part of his park, do not let the Nation surrender forest or hillside, but, preserving them intact, apportion for purposes of cultivation the less beautiful, flatter, and probably more productive ground. Let the public watch how many of the schemes brought forward relate to regulation, not inclosure. Mr. Cross announced, as we have said, that his Bill was intended to promote regulation ; let us watch that its intention is thoroughly fulfilled. The machinery of the Act to regulate commons being now provided, it remains for those who care for open space to see that it is not used to promote inclosure.

Second. The high-handed inclosures for which no Parliamentary sanction is sought, are more difficult to meet. The expense of opposing is considerable ; the legal questions complicated. Few individuals can deal with the problem

single-handed.   Here again, however, happily,
the machinery exists ready to our hands.   The
Commons Preservation Society* was founded
twelve years ago with the express object of
watching over the interests of the public in
the remaining commons of England in Parliament and in the courts of law.   How much
this was needed will be seen when we consider that about 5,000,000 acres have been
inclosed since the reign of Queen Anne, and
that there remain only 1,524,648 acres of open
land, according to the Domesday-book, for all
present and future needs.   The Committee of
this Society gives advice (free from all cost),
to those who wish to consult them respecting
the course to be adopted when open spaces in
their neighbourhood are threatened with inclosure.   If the neighbourhood is poor, and
legal resistance is the only way to meet the
difficulty, the society will, to the best of its
means, aid with money and influence.

* Offices, 1, Great College Street, Westminster.

It appears to me that the objects of this Society are so important and far-reaching that it ought to be a large national union, every one joining it as members and supporting it to the utmost of their power. It is not a question which ought longer to be left to a comparatively few zealous men; it ought to be supported by, and its machinery used by, everyone who cares to keep the common land open. If legal decisions are to be arrived at, if landowners are to be made to feel that they will be called to account for any inclosures made by them, the matter cannot be left in the hands of individuals, and it is only by combination, and under good legal advice, that the undertakings can be rightly and wisely begun and brought to a successful issue.

To meet the third danger—that arising from attempts to obtain compulsory power to purchase small portions of the metropolitan commons supposed to be protected under the Act of 1866—it is important (equally as in

the case of rural commons) to watch each
scheme that may be brought forward, and
thus to let Parliament see that the matter is
one about which the Nation cares. The schemes
previously referred to, relating to commons at
Barnes, Mitcham, and Hampstead, were only
defeated by strenuous public opposition. Under
these schemes it was actually proposed to take
four acres of Barnes Common for a sewage
farm, and to widen the railway that crosses it
by additional sidings and coal depôts; to cut
up Mitcham Common with additional lines of
railway, and to take 100 acres of it for sewage
purposes, and to surround and partly under-
mine Hampstead Heath with a railway provided with three or four stations situated on
some of its prettiest spots!

One other point bearing on the question of
metropolitan commons may be noted here.
Whenever the question of their inclosure has
come up before the courts of law to be tried,
it has been hitherto found that the rights of

commoners have been adjudged sufficient to preserve them from inclosure. It is therefore deeply to be regretted that last session the Board of Works again resorted to their old practice of purchasing these rights; they gave £5,000 for Bostal Heath, near Woolwich. The purchase was clearly unnecessary in this case, because a decree of the Court of Chancery exists preventing the inclosure of the heath. The Board probably took this step from a dislike to the trouble of defending their scheme for regulation. Such a practice must heavily burden the ratepayers of London, already quite sufficiently taxed. And this is done in order to secure for them that which there seems no reason to suppose could not be secured without any such expenditure, open spaces having already been legally preserved without purchase in the cases of Epping, Coulsden, Berkhampstead, and others. It is an old idea of the Metropolitan Board, and not a harmless one. In 1865, the chair-

man and members of the Board proposed to
make the Board the central authority to protect and preserve commons; they asked for
large taxing powers in order to raise money
sufficient to buy up all rights of the lords of
the manors and commoners, and to sell parts
of the metropolitan commons for building, in
order in some degree to recoup the ratepayers.
The committee of the House of Commons
which was then considering the question rejected this scheme of the Metropolitan Board,
holding that the rights of commoners being
amply sufficient to keep the commons open, purchase was unnecessary. This opinion has since
been repeatedly confirmed by decisions in the
law courts. There seems no reason to suppose
that Hampstead Heath, for which the Metropolitan Board gave nearly £50,000, might have
not been kept open without purchase had the
matter been carried to an issue. The question
is an important one as far as the ratepayers
are concerned; it is also very important as a

matter of precedent. The plan of operation of any body of men which, like the Commons Preservation Society, should examine the rights of the public and uphold them by law, is much to be preferred to the purchase scheme, though this may be more acceptable to large land-owners, and have more appearance of magnificence.

To sum up. It is by watchful care that every scheme under the new Act can be well considered and wisely decided when it is brought before Parliament; it is by steady co-operation to bring to a legal issue every unauthorised inclosure that a share in our common land can alone be preserved for the landless classes. Shortly—before, perhaps, as a Nation, we awake to its importance—will this great question be permanently decided.

In England there is a very small and continually decreasing number of landowners. We have no peasant proprietors as in France; and few tenants of small holdings, as in

Ireland. Yet the love of being connected with the land is innate; it deepens a man's attachment to his native country, and adds dignity and simplicity to his character. Each family cannot hope to own a small piece of cultivated land as in France—no inaccessible mountain-ranges exist for our people to learn to love as in Switzerland—but it may be that in our common-land we are meant to learn an even deeper lesson :—something of the value of those possessions in which each of a large community has a distinct share, yet which each enjoys only by virtue of the share the many have in it; in which separate right is subordinated to the good of all; each tiny bit of which would have no value if the surface were divided amongst the hundreds that use it, yet which when owned together and stretching away into loveliest space of heather or forest becomes the common possession of the neighbourhood, or even of the County and Nation. It will give a sense of a common possession to succeeding generations. It will give a share in his country to be inherited by the poorest citizen. It will be a link between the many and through the ages, binding with holy happy recollections those who together have entered into the joys its beauty gives—men and women of different natures, different histories, and different anticipations—into one solemn joyful fellowship, which neither time nor outward change can destroy—as people are bound together by any common memory, or common cause, or common hope.

CHARLES DICKENS AND EVANS, CRYSTAL PALACE PRESS.

By the same Author.

HOMES

OF THE

LONDON POOR.

Extra fcp. 8vo, price 3s. 6d.

"The book should be carefully read by all those whose duties under Mr. Cross's recent Bill are just now commencing."
—*Medical Times.*

"We offer her our hearty commendation, and we trust that her little book will have a wide sale. It is not less interesting than instructive."—*Builder.*

"There are few who have so good a right to be heard on the matter as the author of this volume. She has not only thought long and deeply on the problem to be solved, but she has worked nobly to aid in its solution. . . . We know nothing in literature of this kind more touching than the simple, unaffected tale of her struggles, disappointments, and triumphs. There is not a word of mere sentimentalism in any one of her papers; she is clear, practical, and definite."—*Globe.*

"Miss Octavia Hill has grappled successfully with one of the most difficult and disheartening of our social problems."—*Nonconformist.*

MACMILLAN AND CO., LONDON.

MACMILLAN & CO.'S PUBLICATIONS.

THE SERVICE OF THE POOR. An Enquiry into the Reasons for and against the Establishment of Religious Sisterhoods for Charitable Purposes. By CAROLINE E. STEPHEN. Crown 8vo, 6s. 6d.

"She examines the question patiently and thoroughly, and her book contains much information, and will be useful as a text-book to those who are desirous to use their abilities to the best advantage in the wide and difficult field of philanthropy."—*Athenæum.*

"We recommend Miss Stephen's book to all who are thinking of entering sisterhoods, and still more to all who are engaged in the conduct of them. They will find in it much that deserves consideration, much from which, if they will honestly apply it, they cannot fail to derive profit."—*Saturday Review.*

HOMES OF THE LONDON POOR. By OCTAVIA HILL. Extra fcap. 8vo, 3s. 6d.

"There are few who have so good a right to be heard on the matter as the author of this volume. She has not only thought long and deeply on the problem to be solved, but has worked nobly to aid in its solution. . . . We know nothing in literature of this kind more touching than the simple, unaffected tale of her struggles, disappointments, and triumphs. There is not a word of mere sentimentalism in any one of her papers ; she is clear, practical, and definite."—*Globe.*

STREETS AND LANES OF A CITY. Being the Reminiscences of Amy Dutton ; with a Preface by the Bishop of Salisbury. Second and Cheaper Edition. Extra fcap. 8vo, 2s. 6d.

FIRST LESSONS ON HEALTH. By J. BERNERS. Seventh Edition. 18mo, cloth, 1s.

HOUSEHOLD MANAGEMENT AND COOKERY. By W. B. TEGETMEIER. With an Appendix of Recipes used by the Teachers of the National School of Cookery. 18mo, 1s.

FIRST LESSONS IN THE PRINCIPLES OF COOKING. By LADY BARKER. Second Edition. 18mo, 1s.

MACMILLAN AND CO., LONDON.